The Dumbarton Oaks Conversations and the United Nations 1944–1994

The Dumbarton Oaks Conversations and the United Nations 1944–1994

Ernest R. May
and
Angeliki E. Laiou
editors

DUMBARTON OAKS RESEARCH LIBRARY AND COLLECTION
WASHINGTON, D.C.

Manufactured in the United States of America by
Sheridan Books, Inc., 450 Fame Avenue, Hanover, PA 17331
(717) 632-3535

LIBRARY OF CONGRESS CATALOGING-IN-PUBLICATION DATA

The Dumbarton Oaks conversations and the United Nations, 1944–1994 /
editors, Ernest R. May and Angeliki E. Laiou.
p. cm.
Includes bibliographical references.
ISBN 978-0-88402-255-8 cloth
ISBN 978-0-88402-468-2 paper

1. Dumbarton Oaks Conference (1994).
2. United Nations—History.
I. May, Ernest R. II. Laiou, Angeliki E.
III. Dumbarton Oaks Conference,
1944–1994 (1994 : Washington, D.C.)
JZ4988.D86 1998
341.23'09—dc21

97–48477

EU GPSR Authorised Representative
LOGOS EUROPE, 9 rue Nicolas Poussin, 17000, La Rochelle, France
E-mail: Contact@logoseurope.eu

Contents

Preface to the Twenty-Fifth Anniversary Edition

Why reissue the proceedings of a conference that took place a quarter century ago, which delved into meetings that were convoked in 1944 and into developments in the intervening fifty years? And why make available on the web the catalogue of the exhibition that coincided with the 1994 event?† A little explanation seems in order. As has always proven true in human affairs, much that was once common knowledge has passed out of living memory and needs now to be rehearsed formally. Recollections change as generations do. World War II, a global conflict that began on 1 September 1939, concluded in two stages. The Allied countries formally accepted the unconditional surrender by the armed forces first of Nazi Germany, on 8 May 1945 (Victory in Europe or V-E Day), and then of Imperial Japan, on 2 September 1945 (Victory over Japan or V-J Day).

The term United Nations, coined in the closing days of 1941 and the opening ones of 1942, initially described states committed to victory over Hitlerism and the Axis countries. Eventually the expression developed to designate an international organization, conceived when globalism was ascendant, that would guarantee peace and prosperity to the world. Such an organization mattered hugely after countless millions of lives—both military and civilian—had been lost in six years of total war, genocide, famine, and disease. The creation of the United Nations as a permanent organization held paramount importance to Franklin D. Roosevelt (1882–1945), the thirty-second president of the United States (1933–1945).

Long before the war's end in 1945, delegates from countries around the death-weary world met to think and talk through a framework that could deliver a permanent peace. After all the years of combat and killing, these statesmen were tasked with constituting a new United Nations Organization. They converged at a research institute administered by Harvard University in Washington, D.C. Although since the late 1960s the scope

† www.doaks.org/do-conversations

has been broadened to include other fields, for its first three decades the institution was dedicated solely to the study of Byzantium.

Former residence of United States diplomat Robert Woods Bliss (1875–1962) and his wife, Mildred Barnes Bliss (1879–1969), the site had been given the name Dumbarton Oaks by the couple after they acquired it in 1920. In 1940 they deeded it to Harvard to support an eclectic array of people and programs in the humanities and arts as a civilizing and secluded counterweight to the hustle and bustle of the world outside. Permission to host the meetings came from Harvard University President James B. Conant in Cambridge, but the Blisses themselves supported the decision as well.

The historic mansion and its lovely garden, a breezy island in the haze and humidity of the nation's capital, lent themselves wonderfully to the alternation between large-group and breakout sessions required by a constitutional convention. The small group that arrogated most of the power in the hard negotiations comprised the Big Four: the United States, United Kingdom, Soviet Union, and China. Roosevelt, Churchill, and Stalin fought for their interests by way of proxies. Their policymakers conducted what was in effect a dry run for later meetings to follow elsewhere.

The gatherings, which started on 21 August 1944, and ended on 7 October 1944, were styled the Dumbarton Oaks Conversations. These assemblies led to the release of the so-called Dumbarton Oaks Plan, with an accompanying communiqué, at noon on 9 October 1944. The plan amounted more to proposals than anything else: it was a draft for later discussion, not a text to be voted up or down.

In one sense, the sweep of the participation was momentous. In another, it is easy to reel off the many exclusions. In the group photographs, women can be detected only outside the principal groups, as they hover to the sides or in the rear, not full-fledged participants but part-time assistants. The people of color are almost exclusively African-American servants and entertainers, not participants.

In due course, the cavalcade moved to a different venue. The United Nations Conference on International Organization began in San Francisco on 25 April 1945. Fifty nations signed the Charter of the United Nations on 26 June 1945.

The fiftieth anniversary of the conversations was commemorated at Dumbarton Oaks 5–7 May 1994, in a conference organized by Harvard University faculty members. The commemoration took place a mere two and a half years after the collapse of the Soviet Union in late December 1991. A quarter century later, the world has evolved in ways that would have been unimaginable to many attendees of either the original conversations or the conference. This volume may assist readers who wish to familiarize themselves with the conditions that motivated the meetings in 1944, and the successes and failings of the subsequent organization between 1944 and 1994. Such interested parties may consider the changes that have taken place in the world since then.

A still greater hope is that those who peruse these materials will commit themselves, as they feel best equipped, to maintain collective security and pursue international prosperity without sacrificing peace or other conditions necessary to the preservation of the earth. As obvious as it may sound, we human beings benefit from the exercise of our reason upon knowledge of the past to inform us as we construct a vision of the future.

Jan M. Ziolkowski,
Arthur Kingsley Porter Professor of
Medieval Latin, Harvard University,
and Director of Dumbarton Oaks,
September 2019

Preface

This volume consists of selected papers from the "Dumbarton Oaks Conference, 1944–1994," a gathering held 5–7 May 1994 to celebrate the fiftieth anniversary of the Dumbarton Oaks Conversations, historic meetings that started on 21 August 1944 and established the basis for the United Nations Charter, which was ratified the following year in San Francisco. Many of the issues addressed then remain vital today, and the participants at the 1994 conference discussed both the historical circumstances of the Dumbarton Oaks Conversations and current problems of international relations.

Dumbarton Oaks is a part of Harvard University, and the conference was organized by members of the Harvard faculty: Abram Chayes (Felix Frankfurter Professor of Law, Emeritus), Bryan Hehir (Professor of the Practice in Religion and Society at the divinity school; faculty associate with the Harvard Center for International Affairs [CFIA]; Executive Committee member of the CFIA), Stanley Hoffmann (C. Douglas Dillon Professor of the Civilization of France; chairman of the Center for European Studies), Akira Iriye (Charles Warren Professor of American History), Ernest May (Charles Warren Professor of American History; director of the Charles Warren Center for Studies in American History; professor of history with the John F. Kennedy School of Government; senior research associate at the Center for Science and International Affairs at the Kennedy School), Joseph Nye (dean of the John F. Kennedy School of Government) and Angeliki Laiou (professor of Byzantine history; director of Dumbarton Oaks). Monroe Horn did substantial editorial work on the papers assembled here. Suzanne Mercury made valuable contributions to the preparation of the volume.

Angeliki E. Laiou
Harvard University and
Dumbarton Oaks

Dumbarton Oaks Conference, 1944–1994: Remarks from the Opening Session

Angeliki E. Laiou

Almost fifty years ago, Dumbarton Oaks was the location for the first official talks regarding the formation of international organizations after World War II. At issue were the preservation of peace, prosperity, and national and international security. Those were critical days, and the representatives of the United Kingdom, the Soviet Union, China, and the United States braved the heat and humidity of a Washington summer to meet here from 21 August through 7 October 1944. Indeed, heat was one reason Dumbarton Oaks was chosen: It is one of the coolest spots in Washington. It is also relatively secluded, and the conversations were to be held not secretly, but with little publicity and with maximum security for the delegates. So, for more than six weeks, Dumbarton Oaks was essentially turned over to the State Department and its guests. The Music Room was renamed, for the duration of the conference, the "Assembly Room." The entire first floor was given over to the delegates of the various countries. It is not clear on what principle rooms were allocated to the various delegates, but it must have been considered a graceful gesture to have the Soviet delegation "occupy the room containing the Slavic books." We are told that much of the most fruitful discussion took place on the terrace, in the Orangerie (where lunch was served), over tea, and during walks in the gardens, where the delegates also sometimes cooled themselves off with a swim in the pool. The delegates kept a civilized schedule, 10 A.M. to 5 P.M.

Dumbarton Oaks is a quiet place, dedicated to research. Its usual business is scholarship, a reflective, often introspective pursuit. A certain amount of unworldliness pervades Dumbarton Oaks in normal times, and it can have strange manifestations: In 1942 the air raid shelter was in the Orangerie, surely the only air raid shelter in the world with a glass roof. But the war years brought into willing service both scholars and academic institutions. Indeed, scholarly resources were used with considerable imagination by a generation of statesmen that understood how trained minds function.

Many of my history professors at Harvard, for example, played important and interesting roles in the war. William Langer, the great diplomatic historian, organized and ran the Research and Analysis Branch of the Office of Strategic Services (OSS), recruiting scholars from all sorts of disciplines, from classicists to modernists. My professor of French medieval history worked in this branch, as did my professor of Byzantine history, who was recruited as a very young man and was, as legend has it, the first Westerner to recognize the importance of Tito, which he did by deciphering a garbled intercepted message in Serbo-Croatian. Indeed, much of that section of the OSS was manned by historians, and their reports are a pleasure to read for their analytical sharpness and their elegant reconstructions of distant reality from fragmentary information. One of the scholars who worked at Dumbarton Oaks, Ernst Kitzinger, the eminent historian of Byzantine art, characterized in a telling way the difference between his work as a scholar and his work during the war. In 1944 he was in London, where his main assignment was to evaluate intelligence information regarding the possibility of a last-ditch Nazi stand in the Alps. The methods, he told me, were the same he used when he analyzed sources in his scholarly work; but in 1944, the study had to be done within two weeks, and at the end of it one would know with awful certainty whether the analysis had been right or wrong.

Perhaps the most encouraging type of scholarly involvement that I know about is the work that was undertaken by the National Defense Research Committee. Scholars at Dumbarton Oaks, pursuing their work in Byzantine studies, had been creating archives of Byzantine monuments that were located in various parts of Europe and North Africa. They were now asked to prepare lists of monuments that would be given to the armed forces, so that care would be taken not to bomb them. Since there were two different sets of imperatives here, the preservation of monuments and military objectives, there were, undoubtedly, clashes. But the work went on. The section on Tunisia, for example, was completed in 1943. It is a heartening thought that concern for monuments was an important issue during the war years, although in practice plans did not always meet the task. I am told by Margaret Alexander that in Tunisia a number of little buildings were carefully protected from bombing, because somehow they were thought to be shrines. They were, in fact, tobacco and newspaper kiosks.

There was, everyone agrees, a spirit of optimism at the start of what was officially called "The Washington Conversations on International Organization," which began formally on that 21 August at 10:30 A.M. This optimism was reflected in the opening statements of Secretary of State Cordell Hull: "to create the institutional foundations for a just and enduring peace"; Soviet ambassador Andrei Gromyko: "[The freedom-loving peoples of the world] are striving to establish an international organization [to] . . . guarantee for the peoples peace, security and prosperity in the future"; Chinese ambassador V. K. Wellington Koo: "we owe it to [the freedom-loving peoples] as well as to humanity at large to subordinate all other considerations to the achievements of our common object"; and Sir Alexander Cadogan's hope that "humanity may find the way to a better and nobler life."[1] At the close of the conference, both President Franklin Roosevelt and Secretary Hull expressed great pleasure with the results. What the expectations were, in August 1944, and whether they were realized, is a topic that will be addressed here by eminent specialists. That the conversations were important, however, I think cannot be denied. Many of the issues that were at the forefront during the entire postwar period were raised and discussed, to a greater or lesser extent, at Dumbarton Oaks—issues of social and economic cooperation, including educational and cultural problems; human rights and sexual equality; the peaceful resolution of disputes; and issues of security. Fundamental problems regarding regional versus international organizations, national sovereignty, and international structures were all analyzed, although few were truly resolved.

Many of these questions have acquired a new urgency in our time, when the global situation has evolved in a way that poses grave challenges to international institutions as well as to individual states; this is a time in which the dynamic between national sovereignty and the needs or perceived needs of international security (broadly conceived) changes every day, demanding new answers on both the theoretical and the practical level. We live in a world in transition, where there is evident tension between

[1] *Washington Conversations on International Organization, Dumbarton Oaks, 1944* (Washington, D.C.: Government Printing Office, 1945), 3 ff.

processes of fragmentation on the one hand, and the building of large regional and global units on the other. We live in a time of fragile prosperity for some and great suffering for many. The historians among us know that such periods of transition are not unique. Some of us, in the normal course of events, recognize both fragmentation and restructuring as processes that in the past have often resulted in the creation of new viable units that offered greater peace, security, and prosperity than the units they replaced. This happens often, but not always. Perhaps an important difference between the past and the present is that now we do have international institutions. Their function and role seem to be among the most vital questions of our day, but, even as demands on international institutions are increasing, the answers are far from obvious.

At this critical juncture, it seems timely to examine what the role of international institutions has been, and what new imperatives might lie ahead. "Dumbarton Oaks Conference, 1944–1994" was conceived not as a retrospective but as a forum where the present and the future would also be discussed. Many of the topics that appear on the program were topics that were raised at the conversations in 1944; they continue to be as vital now as they were then.

In the concluding chapter of *Dumbarton Oaks: The Origins of the United Nations and the Search for Postwar Security,* Robert Hilderbrand wonders why, given the political difficulties and developing antagonisms, the 1944 Dumbarton Oaks Conversations had a certain success. Undoubtedly part of the answer lies in hard work and a willingness to compromise, but another of the reasons, Hilderbrand adduces, is the "spectacular place" in which they were held, and the fact that the meetings "had been too heavily publicized to be permitted to fail."[2] The 1994 conference, fortunately, is held in peaceful times—at least by comparison—and its tasks are certainly different from those of 1944. But I hope that the spirit of the place will bless fruitful discussion—the first set of discussions and reflection in what undoubtedly will be a series of meetings as the anniversaries of Bretton Woods and San Francisco approach. Important issues will, I hope, be aired here and contribute to the debate.

We owe the intellectual organization of this conference to the collec-

[2] Robert Hilderbrand, *Dumbarton Oaks: The Origins of the United Nations and the Search for Postwar Security* (Chapel Hill: University of North Carolina Press, 1990), 247.

tive genius of the members of the organizing committee—my colleagues at Harvard. Professor Ernest May and I discussed the possibility of such a meeting close to two years ago. His encouragement and his great expertise moved the matter from a thought to reality. The road to realization was paved by the organizing committee as a whole, in a series of meetings that were as intellectually stimulating as they were pleasant. I should like to thank Professors Abram Chayes, Bryan Hehir, Stanley Hoffmann, Akira Iriye, Ernest May, and Joseph Nye for having made this conference possible. We owe a special word of thanks to President Neil Rudenstine for the enthusiastic support he gave this project from the beginning.

On behalf of the organizing committee, I should like to thank our eminent speakers and moderators, who have come from near and far for this conference. For help and advice, I thank the members of the Honorary Committee. We are indebted to a number of other friends, among them Ambassador Arthur Hartman and Mr. Marvin Moss.

Members of the staff of Dumbarton Oaks have worked hard to make this a successful conference. I should like to thank Joachim Wolschke-Bulmahn and Linda Lott of the landscape architecture program for mounting an exhibition with photographs and documents from 1944. Susan Boyd and Stephen Zwirn, curator and assistant curator of the Byzantine collection, have overseen the transformation of the Courtyard Gallery into an elegant conference room. Carol Sellery and Kinsey Katchka of the Director's Office have worked with great dedication, and I thank them. Cynthia Pinkston and all the knowledgeable and loyal docents and volunteers have offered their time and expertise with enthusiasm. I am grateful to Suzanne Mercury, whom most of the speakers have come to know well. She has lived with this project for more than a year, nurturing it with imagination, affection, and efficiency. Without her efforts it would not have materialized.

Angeliki E. Laiou

Postscript

The "Dumbarton Oaks Conference, 1944–1994" began with a reception at the State Department, where Douglas J. Bennet, US assistant secretary of state for International Organization Affairs, gave the keynote address, raising historical as well as actual issues. He asked,

> Did the founders of the UN have a vision? Were they pragmatists simply trying to avoid further conflagration? Or were they an inspired combination of the two? In any such human undertaking, there must have been a mixture of hope, hype, hubris, courage, and necessity. There was a profound sense of the Allied cause rolling full force toward victory. There was optimism: Cordell Hull, anticipating the debate to come between Dumbarton Oaks and San Francisco, wrote: "It is, of course, inevitable that when many governments and peoples attempt to agree on a single plan the result will be in terms of the highest common denominator rather than the plan of any one nation." There was clearly the courage to decide—to sign off on fundamental issues such as whether human rights and self-determination should be in the Charter. Of course there was vision—enough vision to imagine a world without war in which individual rights were protected. There was enough commitment, urgency, confidence, and authority to put out a draft, take views, and ratify the Charter of a new world organization nine months later.

Bennet also spoke of the importance of the Cold War:

> The Dumbarton Oaks institutions were not designed to deal with it and were slowly paralyzed when it came. They were increasingly marginalized in the eyes of the founding nations because they could not contribute decisively to security. At the same time, however, they did provide a forum and structure for the new states emerging from colonialism.

In the wake of the Cold War, Bennet stressed the need for fresh interpretations of "the forces driving today's world and . . . a fresh infusion of vision and commitment."

US senators Nancy Landon Kassebaum and Paul Sarbanes, speaking on the final day of the conference, raised issues of policy in its national and international complexity. Senator Kassebaum noted, "Nearly every nation is undergoing this same sort of challenge to the trust in their institutions, and they can be local, state, or federal. We have to somehow renew that trust." She went on to say,

> Today people want to feel positive and secure, but also they really want to be able to do it in the context of the reality that they see around them. . . . And what are the overarching problems that we must try to face? Some have been mentioned earlier that were not touched on fifty years ago and they are ones we need to address for the twenty-first century—which means beginning right now. The environment is one; overpopulation another; and the refugee problem, which . . . was not really thought of in the context of Dumbarton Oaks. This is a particular problem in Africa. There have always been somewhat nomadic movements, but nothing, nothing on the scale and the trauma of what is taking place today: massive movements of population back and forth.

Senator Sarbanes, noting that the end of the Cold War gives the world the opportunity to put into practice "much of what [the Dumbarton Oaks Conversations] had been anticipating," asked the fundamental question of whether the existing structures are adequate or whether they are insufficient and need to be changed. Mentioning three areas that affect the functioning of international institutions—resources, personnel, and management—he concluded,

> It is my own view that what is needed is to try to maximize the utilizations of these institutions and organizations. That is where the focus should go now, rather than [toward] a restructuring of them. . . . With the implosion of the Soviet Union, we have an opportunity that is unparalleled in the post-World War II period. We face a challenge which historians will examine and place a very serious judgment upon if we do not maximize our opportunities in the current context.

The papers that follow seek to illuminate some of the major issues that have engaged international institutions since 1944.

Opening Remarks: Dumbarton Oaks Conference, 1944–1994

Neil L. Rudenstine

It may seem anomalous for this extraordinarily beautiful setting—an important university center for the study of Byzantine, medieval, and other cultures—to have served as a place for the most serious possible discussions concerning war and the prospects for peace. In fact, however, the conversations that were carried on here in 1944—among representatives of the United Kingdom, the Soviet Union, the United States, and, later, China—were much more in keeping with the fundamental purposes of Dumbarton Oaks, and even its preexisting uses, than we might suspect. I would like to take a few moments to focus on that small corner of the large and complex terrain to be explored here.

Mr. and Mrs. Robert Woods Bliss generously deeded Dumbarton Oaks to Harvard University in 1940. Mr. Bliss was himself a diplomat and student of international affairs. In 1919, he and his wife began looking for a home in Washington, and someone suggested to them a place called "The Oaks." In a speech to the Harvard Club of Washington on 8 April 1943, Mr. Bliss recalled that the property had been, in his words, "very much down at the heel, and though it had no particular charm and the grounds were unkempt and in places much overgrown, the beautiful trees gave promise of possibilities." The Blisses eventually decided they could—in Mr. Bliss's phrase—"find [a] way to make the old house and noble trees productive of beauty and enlightenment."[1]

In time, the Blisses resolved to convert their house into more than a home. They decided to make it, in Mr. Bliss's words, "a vital centre of distinguished and productive scholarship, . . . a continuing haven for seek-

[1] Transcript of speech, Dumbarton Oaks.

ers after truth." And so, Dumbarton Oaks became part of Harvard, following the expressed intention that is inscribed on the plaque outside this building: that this scholarly center, by promoting a deeper understanding of the past, would help "to clarify an everchanging present and to inform the future with wisdom."

That transfer took place in 1940. Within two years—by 1942—the United States was of course at war, and in 1942 Dumbarton Oaks had become not only a place for medieval and Byzantine scholarship, but also a locus for wartime research. The National Defense Research Committee had taken over part of the main building. In his 1943 speech to the Harvard Club, Mr. Bliss said he was deeply gratified that Dumbarton Oaks was being used to make a direct contribution to the war effort, but he could not help remarking on what he called the "strange juxtaposition" of activities occurring within his former home. "One half of the building," he said, "is devoted to evolving means to kill human beings more speedily and in greater numbers; the other half continues to develop greater knowledge of the artistic creation of man. One works for the development of the most hideous activity of war, the other for the discovery and preservation of the beauty of human expression."

As the former home of a distinguished diplomat, and as a place where research focused on war was carried on beside scholarship focused on the creative capacity of the human imagination, Dumbarton Oaks was quite a fitting setting for the conversations that occurred here in 1944—conversations intended to see beyond the machinery of destruction, and to develop a framework that might contribute to the furtherance of peace among different peoples and nations of the world.

As we know, the discussions that took place here fifty years ago did not, in themselves, *produce* the United Nations. They were preliminary and exploratory, and the joint statement issued at the conclusion of the talks frankly described the results as "tentative proposals" that would need "further study" in order to serve as a "complete" basis for a more comprehensive conference to form a new international organization. In this sense, too, those first talks and their tentative results may well seem altogether consistent with the nature and purposes of an academic research center—a place where proposals are perhaps invariably tentative, and where "further study" is virtually an absolute requirement of the organism itself. But if this concept of unwavering provisionality and the commitment to continuous analysis and further study seem like occupational hazards peculiarly academic in nature, those in the academy—and perhaps all of us—can take some real comfort from the fact that the original conversations (and the 1944 joint statement) were of course the creation of government representatives and diplomats concerned primarily to reach *definitive* conclusions and to take tangible actions.

Conclusions and actions did, fortunately, occur within the following year. As we know, however, even those subsequent steps did not solve everything, and did not vitiate—either then or now—the absolute need for more reflection, questioning, probing, and constant searching for solutions to underlying problems that remain with us today, and will in some sense always be with us: What patterns do we see in international and human relations that lead us, over and over again, to open conflict and war, rather than peace? What are the conditions that seem to allow for successful interventions and resolutions, and which situations remain intractable, baffling, impenetrable? How can we learn from the complex strands of our past experience, in ways that might be effective in helping to shape our experience in the future?

These are political questions, but they are also economic, psychological, social, religious, cultural, and military in nature. They are questions for people in government who must lead and act; but they also require intense study and the most profound, searching, imaginative analysis—never to be finished. In this sense, these questions are precisely what universities are committed to exploring, and to answering, however provisionally. I am pleased, therefore, that Dumbarton Oaks, Harvard University, the United Nations, and our common stake in curative and healing international action—illuminated by ceaseless and devoted study—should come together in just this place, at another significant moment in the world's history.

Harvard University

The United Nations: From War Fighting to Peace Planning

Michael Howard

Here, where the sword United Nations drew,
Our countrymen were warring on that day!
And this is much—and all—which will not pass away!

It was with this Byronic quotation that Winston Churchill greeted President Franklin Roosevelt's choice of the term "United Nations" to describe the twenty-six nations which, by the beginning of 1942, had joined forces to fight Hitler and his allies.[1] Churchill himself had originally preferred to call them the "Grand Alliance," in memory of the alliance of European states that his ancestor the Duke of Marlborough had led against the France of Louis XIV. The word "alliance," however, would have caused constitutional problems for the United States, and Roosevelt considered that the term "Associated Powers," used in the World War I, would sound too flat. So it was as "The United Nations" that the allies issued their first declaration on New Year's Day 1942, and it was of course a declaration not of peace but of war. The Germans stood at the gates of Moscow, and their submarines were dominating the Atlantic, while the Japanese were overrunning the Philippines and Southeast Asia. The signatories simply pledged themselves to employ their full resources in the prosecution of the war, to cooperate with one another, and not to conclude any separate armistice or peace. For most of them, the unity of the United Nations was the condition for their survival.

[1] Winston S. Churchill, *The Second World War,* vol. 4, *The Hinge of Fate* (London: Cassell, 1951), 605.

But in the preamble to that declaration, the signatories stated that they had "subscribed to a common program of purposes and principles embodied in the joint declaration of the President of the United States and the Prime Minister of the United Kingdom . . . dated August 14, 1941, known as the Atlantic Charter." That document had laid out a vision of a postwar world in which all nations could freely choose the form of government under which they would live, would have equal access to trade and raw materials needed for their prosperity, would collaborate in improving their standards of living, would be able to traverse the high seas without let or hindrance, and "for realistic as well as spiritual reasons . . . come to the abandonment of the use of force." Aggressor nations would therefore be disarmed, it declared, "pending the establishment of a wider system of general security."[2]

This vision of the postwar world was quintessentially American. The British disliked some of it, and were skeptical about most of it. For them, the important thing was to get the Americans on board—first as allies in fighting the war, and then as associates in keeping a peace founded on effective guarantees that aggressor nations such as Nazi Germany and Imperial Japan would not trouble the world again. But the government of the United States had a more comprehensive vision of what would be involved in creating a more peaceful world. Almost uniquely among belligerent nations, it had started to plan the peace even before it had entered the war. As soon as war broke out in Europe, in September 1939, Cordell Hull, Roosevelt's secretary of state, set up committees to make postwar plans for such matters as economic cooperation, political organization, and disarmament. The content of the Atlantic Charter very closely reflected that thinking.

When the United Nations signed up behind the principles of the Atlantic Charter, it was accepting, with greater or lesser degrees of conviction, the American model for the postwar world. But notice how cautiously the charter treated the question of an international organization to preserve security. It merely expressed the expectation that one should eventually be established. In fact, Churchill had pressed for the inclusion of a reference to an "effective international organization," but Roosevelt had

[2] Ruth B. Russell, *A History of the United Nations Charter: The Role of the United States, 1940–1945* (Washington, D.C.: Brookings Institution, 1958), 975.

demurred "because of the suspicions and opposition that such a statement on his part would create in the United States."[3] It continued to be a contentious issue throughout the war, and Roosevelt knew that he must tread a very narrow path between the extreme internationalists and the traditional isolationists in a hostile and suspicious Congress if he was not to suffer the fate of President Woodrow Wilson in 1919.

Yet in the planning for the postwar world that was set on foot both in Washington and in London in 1942, the question of an international organization—its membership, structure, and powers—became quite central, and a huge amount of documentation was accumulated about it by hard-working officials. At this stage, however, the value of their work was circumscribed by the fact that those working on the project had no contact with one another and little more with their own political leaders. Gladwyn Jebb, the Foreign Office official mainly responsible for drafting the British proposals, started out with the assumption that it would be necessary to curb American aspirations to world hegemony. If the Americans took the lead, he reflected, "might not the rest of the world regard the system as a sort of anonymous Anglo-Saxon tyranny? . . . We should not give the impression that we wanted to transform La Beauce into a sort of Manitoba, and construct another Pittsburgh on the ruins of the Ruhr." In any case, he reported gloomily, Winston Churchill "was quite allergic to any proposals that he had not himself engendered."[4] As for Roosevelt, he wanted to postpone any public discussion of the question for as long as he could to avert the domestic disruption that he feared it might cause, and so he gave the State Department even less to go on.

By 1943, postponement was no longer possible. The landings in North Africa and the Soviet victory at Stalingrad made Allied victory appear no longer a remote aspiration, but only a matter of time. Churchill himself, in the immediate aftermath of the Casablanca Conference in January, set out his own views of a postwar world where aggression would be held in check by a continuing alliance of the United Kingdom, the United States, and the Soviet Union, who together would form the nucleus of a World Council, while regional councils for Europe, the Pacific and the American

[3] Russell, *United Nations Charter,* 388.

[4] Gladwyn Jebb, *The Memoirs of Lord Gladwyn* (London: Weidenfeld and Nicolson, 1972), 114–18.

Hemisphere would be responsible for settling disputes within their own territories. These ideas he floated when he visited Washington in May 1943, and found them not too far distant from those held by President Roosevelt. The president went even further in desiring the continuance of a Great Power hegemony by urging that the whole world should be disarmed except for the "Four Policemen"—the fourth being China, an addition about which the British felt rather skeptical but in which they politely acquiesced.

Meanwhile, Gladwyn Jebb and his Foreign Office colleagues had visited Washington in March 1943—most of them had never been to America in their lives—and were delighted to find not only that their opposite numbers at the State Department, such as Leo Pasvolsky, Norman Davis, and James Dunn, were as intelligent and frustrated as they were themselves (if better informed), but that they also shared many of their views and problems, including those of obtaining access to their political leaders and restraining some of their wilder ideas. None of them liked Churchill's desire for regional councils, or Roosevelt's nakedly hegemonic ambitions. The British in particular, who were negotiating not only on their own behalf but on that of their partners in the Commonwealth, were anxious to mitigate the difference in power and responsibility between the Great Powers and their smaller allies. But all this was small print compared with the agreement they had reached in principle about the need to establish some kind of international organization, and the British noted that everyone in Washington was already calling it the "United Nations."

In the summer of 1943, Roosevelt decided that the time had come to go public on the issue, largely, he told Churchill at the Quebec Conference in August, to preempt any propaganda that his political opponents might make about the matter during the run-up to the presidential election the following year. The support of the Soviet Union was enlisted when Secretary Hull and the British foreign secretary, Anthony Eden, visited Moscow in October. The evolution of Soviet thinking about postwar cooperation awaits its historian. Perhaps at this stage there was not any; Stalin had other things on his mind. For him the main purpose of the conference was to ensure that the Anglo-American second front would be opened the following spring as promised, but he acquiesced in the inclusion, in the subsequent declaration, of a clause recognizing "the necessity of establishing at the earliest practicable date a general international organization, based on the principle of the sovereign equality of all peace-loving states, and open to membership by all such states, large and small, for the maintenance of international peace and security."[5] No doubt he felt about it what many British had felt about the Atlantic Charter: such high-sounding declarations had all too little to do with the urgent business of getting on with the war, but if they ensured the cooperation of powerful allies there was no harm in making them.

After the Moscow declaration, planning for the new international organization went into high gear. The Soviets indeed suggested that this should be done jointly, but Roosevelt, again fearful of the domestic implications of this, preferred that for the moment each government should proceed separately, but keep closely in touch. But early in January 1944, Secretary Hull gave notice that he proposed to convene a four-power conference specifically to discuss the issue, and on 30 May the invitations were issued for senior officials to assemble for an "informal" conference in Washington the coming August. So in August 1944, the delegates duly assembled at Dumbarton Oaks; that is, the delegates of the United States, the United Kingdom, and the Soviet Union. Since the Soviet Union was not as yet at war with Japan and so did not regard itself as an ally of the Republic of China, a second phase of the talks was arranged which the Chinese would attend and the Soviets would not.

By this time, the State Department had worked out detailed proposals for the structure of the United Nations, with which the British found themselves very largely in agreement. "Very good," commented Sir Alexander Cadogan, the head of the Foreign Office and leader of the British delegation, when he saw them, "except that there is a good deal about 'territorial trusteeship!' "[6] The purpose of the organization was defined as being "*first,* to maintain international security and peace, and *second,* to foster through international co-operation the conditions of stability and well-being necessary for peaceful and friendly relations among nations and essential to the maintenance of security and peace."[7] The plan for the organization was very much that subsequently adopted. There was to be a Gen-

[5] Russell, *United Nations Charter,* 977–78.

[6] Alexander Cadogan, *The Diaries of Sir Alexander Cadogan, 1938–45,* ed. David Dilks (London: Cassell, 1971), 650.

[7] Russell, *United Nations Charter,* 996.

eral Assembly; an Executive Council of eleven states, of which seven were to be annually elected with the four Great Powers as permanent members; an International Court of Justice; and a permanent Secretariat. Procedures were laid down for the peaceful settlement of disputes, with possible enforcement action, and for general economic cooperation.

There was no problem accepting the American proposals as the working documents for the conference, and the bulk of them were accepted with remarkable speed and amity. The Soviet delegates, when one considers their previous and subsequent records, were models of friendly cooperation. Their leader was Andrei Gromyko, whom the West was to come to know all too well over the next thirty years, but whom Cadogan considered to be "a very nice and sensible fellow."[8] Jebb described him in more detail as "imperturbable, sardonic, scrupulous, humorless, and formidably exact."[9] The Soviets made trouble over only two issues: their demand that all sixteen republics of the Soviet Union should enjoy full membership in the organization, and that the Great Powers should exercise an effective veto over questions affecting their own interests.

Neither of these matters could be settled at Dumbarton Oaks, but both were later resolved at the Yalta summit the following spring. The question of membership was probably no more than an opening bid, and in view of the number of members who might at the time be seen as effectively client states of the Anglo-Saxon powers, it was an understandable attempt to secure something like voting equality. As for the veto, both the United Kingdom and the United States had at one stage considered such a provision desirable. Secretary Hull indeed had assured Congress that the veto power "was chiefly for the benefit of the United States in the light of the world situation and our own public opinion."[10] Within a few years, both the United Kingdom and the United States were to find the right of veto an essential element in the conduct of their own policies and had good cause to bless the Soviet Union for having brought it into being. It cannot therefore be said that the Soviets were using either issue to wreck the conference. Gladwyn Jebb, whose subsequent experience was to rival

[8] Cadogan, *Diaries,* 659.

[9] Jebb, *Memoirs,* 149.

[10] Cordell Hull, *The Memoirs of Cordell Hull,* 2 vols. (London: Hodder and Stoughton, 1948), 2:1662.

even that of Gromyko, later wrote that "a unique feature of this conference was that it was the only one in which the Russians took part with hardly any apparent *arrières pensées* and with an obviously sincere will to reach agreement."[11]

These were indeed halcyon days. In the West, the German front in Normandy had broken, the Allies had landed in the south of France, Paris had been liberated, and Allied forces were pouring into Belgium and Holland. In the East, Soviet soil was being cleared of the invading forces, and Germany's allies—Finland, Romania, and Bulgaria—were suing for peace. A spirit of high euphoria reigned, comparable only to that when the Berlin Wall crumbled and the Soviet Union collapsed a few years ago. It was generally realized that the future peace of the world depended on the continuation of Great Power solidarity. As Hull himself had put it a few months earlier, "Without an enduring understanding between these four nations upon their fundamental purposes, interests and obligations to one another, all organizations to preserve peace are creations on paper, and the path is wide open again for the rise of a new aggressor."[12] In August 1944 such an enduring understanding seemed entirely possible.

It is indeed surprising that the United Nations should have survived as well as it has once that understanding had dissolved. That only shows how solid were the foundations laid by our predecessors when they met at Dumbarton Oaks fifty years ago.

[11] Jebb, *Memoirs,* 149.

[12] Hull, *Memoirs,* 2: 1651.

Sober Expectations: The United Nations and a "Sensible Machinery" for Peace

Dorothy V. Jones

One of the most striking things about the Dumbarton Oaks Conversations is the lack of argument that there was in 1944–45 on the basic question of whether there should be an international organization of some kind to help keep the peace after World War II. The broad agreement implied by the phrase "lack of argument" does not mean universal agreement, of course. There were those who sympathized with the views of people such as Gerald L. K. Smith, even if they did not—as he did—show up at the gates of Dumbarton Oaks one day at an early stage in the meetings, making a lot of noise and demanding that "true nationalists" be admitted to the meetings in order to defend America against the imposition of a super state, and then, having reaped a harvest of publicity, departing for greener pastures.

Putting such antics aside, we are left with a truly remarkable unanimity of feeling and purpose. It is particularly remarkable when set against the background of the debates that accompanied the establishment of the League of Nations. The bitterness and divisiveness of those debates made them a lesson to be avoided. This, of course, helps to explain much that happened in 1944–45. Memories of what had happened in the past hung heavily over the proceedings at Dumbarton Oaks and, later, in San Francisco.

The dominant view at both locations, but especially at Dumbarton Oaks, was based on a very narrowly focused reading of the past. In that reading, the past was seen as a set of mistakes that must not be repeated. First, the public had to be prepared to support the establishment of an international organization, and this had to be done well in advance. Woodrow Wilson's desperate last-minute speaking tour to rally support for the league was not for these leaders. Second, the United States and the Soviet Union had to be full and active members right from the start. Third, the Great Powers had to agree at the outset to act together through the international organization to resist aggression. Fourth, the organization itself needed more effective enforcement mechanisms than the league ever had.

The past—or, rather, this particular reading of the past—was not all that hung over the proceedings at Dumbarton Oaks and in San Francisco; there was also what was then the present, with all of its complications. There was the question of Poland, the difficulty of which was symbolized at Dumbarton Oaks at the opening session in August 1944 in the Music Room. A large portrait of Paderewski was taken out of the room before the meeting opened, lest this reminder of Polish patriotism offend the Soviets. Other contemporary problems included voting, membership, trusteeship, and the status of China.

Here, too, we have an apt symbol for these difficulties. In the Edward R. Stettinius, Jr. papers at the University of Virginia there is a photograph to which we might give the caption, "An Exceedingly Awkward Affair." On one weekend, Stettinius, who was the ranking member of the US delegation, decided to try to ease relationships among the delegates. Informal contacts were to do the trick, so he took the delegates on a tour of historic and scenic sites in Virginia. Along the way, they stopped for a picnic lunch. The photograph shows eight delegates seated in full sunshine on a grassy hillside, feet braced to keep from slipping down the slope, lunches balanced on their knees, everyone in full suit and tie, and everyone except the host looking as if he would rather be anywhere else.

Theirs was an awkward balancing act of more than just their lunches. Members of the Chinese, British, and American delegations were there on that sunny hillside. Since the Chinese were there, that meant that the Soviets were not. This also meant that the Soviet party had to be escorted separately on the tour. So, at a decent diplomatic distance from the Chinese, the Soviets saw Virginia, but they went sightseeing without the ranking member of their delegation, Andrei Gromyko, who wisely chose to remain in Washington.

Nowhere is the weight of the past and of what was then the present more obvious than in the address of President Harry Truman at the opening of the United Nations Conference in San Francisco on 25 April 1945. Truman was no orator, and he knew it, just as he knew that he was not prepared for the job into which he had been thrust only thirteen days earlier by the death of Franklin Roosevelt. *Un*patrician, *un*polished, *un*-almost everything that Roosevelt had been, Truman still struggled to fill the presidential shoes and do what he thought was right. He believed in the need for an international organization, and in flat, uninspiring prose, he added his voice to those warning that the world must not repeat the mistakes of the past. "The essence of our problem here," he told the delegates in San Francisco, "is to provide sensible machinery for the settlement of disputes among nations."[1]

It is from Truman's statement that I have taken part of the title for this chapter. I have taken it because it expresses the mood as well as the expectations of many at the time. The mood, particularly at San Francisco after the death of Roosevelt, was one of somber determination. This time they would be "sensible." They would learn from the past. They would build power into an international structure, and that power would enable the organization to keep the peace. The League of Nations had failed to do so, but at San Francisco they would not—they dared not—fail again. Another war would be too horrible to contemplate—although they did contemplate it, rhetorically, again and again, and used the nightmare vision as a spur to keep themselves at their labors.

In summary, at Dumbarton Oaks we have one set of expectations about the future and about the organization that was to ensure that it would be a peaceful one. We have full and active membership of the United States and the Soviet Union, Great Power cooperation, and enforcement mechanisms. From this set of expectations, we have the Dumbarton Oaks Proposals.

At San Francisco, in the spring of 1945, a different set of expectations about the future of the international system came to the surface and demanded attention. In the end, this set of expectations affected the writing of the United Nations Charter and, thus, the future of the organization. These expectations, like those of the Great Powers, were based on a reading of the past that sought lessons for the present. The reading was wider than that of the Great Powers, however, and it looked farther into the past.

[1] Harry S. Truman, "Address to the Opening Session of the United Nations Conference on International Organization," 25 April 1945, *Documents of the United Nations Conference on International Organization, San Francisco, 1945,* vol. 1 (London-New York: United Nations Information Organizations, 1945), doc. 8, G/5, 114.

It did not stop in 1919 with the establishment of the League of Nations. It looked back to the Hague Conferences of 1899 and 1907, and beyond that to the efforts of such private organizations as the Institute of International Law and the Inter-Parliamentary Union to establish rules for the conduct of nation-states.

In contrast to the power-based expectations that dominated the conversations at Dumbarton Oaks, at Yalta, and, to a large extent, at San Francisco as well, these expectations were not based on power: They were based on principles and on rules derived from those principles. Those who held these expectations did not despise power—far from it. Since many of the states which brought these matters to the fore were lesser powers, they were keenly aware of the role that political and military power played in international affairs. This was particularly true in Latin America, where the rule-based tradition of thought about international affairs was very strong and where the power of the United States was a presence felt in every foreign ministry.

The rule-based tradition held that power was not enough. Even peace was not enough—at least, not peace *per se.* The question was, what kind of peace were the allied United Nations trying to achieve and maintain? It was all very well to say "peace with justice," but that did not answer the question; it only opened up a whole new argument about the requirements of justice. This was not, however, a trackless field; people had been making trails of agreement across it for years—agreements that could not be ignored in the establishment of the new organization that was to keep the peace. Many of the lesser states at San Francisco were the ones to notice, for example, that the word "justice" did not even appear in the first two chapters of the Dumbarton Oaks Proposals, where the purposes and principles of the organization were supposed to be set out.

After the meetings at Dumbarton Oaks, the Great Powers circulated the proposals to the rest of the allied nations for comments and recommendations. They were careful to say that nothing was final and that these were only suggestions. There was not the slightest chance, however, that the opinions of, say, Costa Rica or Liberia would make any difference at all in the assignment of permanent seats on the Security Council. As everyone knew, the Great Powers held all the high cards. They also, as the smaller powers freely acknowledged, took most of the high-stake risks. The Great Powers did not hold *all* the cards, however, and they were not the only players in the game—as became clear at San Francisco in the spring of 1945.

The United Nations Charter signed on 26 June 1945 differed in many respects from the proposals that had been hammered out at Dumbarton Oaks: Security arrangements were fleshed out; procedures in voting were defined with a minuteness worthy of medieval scholastics; a whole section on trusteeship was added; a preamble was written and put into place. There were also some significant additions to the chapter on purposes and principles and to the chapter on international economic and social cooperation.

Representatives of fifty nations signed the Charter in San Francisco. Forty nations had provided written comments on the Dumbarton Oaks Proposals in which they laid out their own expectations for the organization and for the future whose peace it was to maintain. It is in these comments, as well as in the speeches of many of the delegates from the smaller powers, that the rule-based tradition of thought can be seen. At San Francisco, its adherents demanded—and received—references to justice, international law, equality, self-determination, political independence, territorial integrity, non-intervention, fundamental freedoms, and basic human rights "without distinction as to race, sex, language, or religion."[2]

Some of these principles derived from very old traditions of thought about society and about the relations of human beings to each other and to their governments. Others came from attempts in the late nineteenth and early twentieth centuries to set out principles and rules applicable to the behavior of states rather than individuals. These rules would—in the best case—guide state behavior. Failing that, they would at least provide standards by which behavior could be judged. Many groups in many countries had worked for years on these matters. Their efforts were often organized as a set of principles and rules entitled, "The Rights and Duties of States."

This tradition of thought affected the writing of the league covenant, and, much more directly and obviously, the writing of the UN Charter. (Incidentally, the same concerns would surface in 1970 in the Declaration of Principles of International Law concerning Friendly Relations and Co-operation among States.) Justice, international law, the rights and duties of states, basic human rights, fundamental freedoms—all of these reflected a

[2] UN Charter, Article 1, paragraph 3.

set of expectations about the United Nations that, if not as strong as the expectations about security arrangements that dominated the discussions at Dumbarton Oaks, were still strong and persistent enough to merit inclusion in the Charter. They should, therefore, merit inclusion in any study of the United Nations as an active institution.

It is tempting to put these two sets of expectations—the power-based and the rule-based—into the familiar dichotomy of realism and idealism. It is perhaps more useful to look at them in a different way, not as a set of opposites but, rather, as complementary approaches to the same goal: peace. Peace, as it was seen in 1944–45, was to be made secure through power collectively applied. Peace was also to be made worthwhile through a collective effort to realize all the principles we might gather together and express in the one word: "justice."

So, then, the expectations of 1944–45 were in one sense rather restrained; that is why I used the word "sober" in my title. The League of Nations had failed to prevent war. The war in which the nations were still engaged at the time of the Dumbarton Oaks Conversations and the San Francisco Conference was more than enough to stimulate sober thoughts all around. At the same time, those expectations aimed rather high; the "sensible machinery" for peace that came out of the lengthy deliberations at Dumbarton Oaks and in San Francisco recognized the importance of principles as well as power, of justice as well as security. Even a casual consideration of the Charter would conclude that the balance between such goals is an unstable one. But then, hasn't it always been?

A Strategic Triad for the New Era

Vladimir Petrovsky

International politics has always been one of the most vibrant, dynamic, and difficult-to-predict spheres of human activity. However, the singularity of the contemporary political situation is that change is taking place on an unprecedented scale. The current transformation of the international political system is occurring exceptionally quickly and comprehensively, involving social, political, economic, as well as cultural aspects. We are witnessing a shift in the civilizational paradigm; in the transition from a technogenic to predominantly anthropogenic civilization, the major role will be played not only by political units, such as states and their governments, but also by individuals. This is a global process, the consequences of which are not yet clear. To discern its scale and major directions, we need to select a few key notions that can help us see the outlines of the whole picture. I would like to suggest three such key notions: security—one of the major conceptual concerns of the international community; multilateralism—the main tool for interaction in conditions of interdependence; and leadership—the factor of political will, which to a considerable extent determines the shaping of the future. These notions also indicate the principal course of action to be taken by the international community to influence the process of change and to direct it into evolutionary, non-violent, and democratic channels.

Perhaps the most important feature of the social sciences in general and of political philosophy in particular is the way their vocabulary is formed. In the natural sciences, we have precise and reliable definitions, from the time of Euclid onward, the terms "oval" or "square" have always had the same meaning. In the social sphere, however, the situation is entirely different. Social and political phenomena are fluid, ever-changing, without well-defined boundaries or permanent attributes. It is extremely difficult to define a social phenomenon—and, having arrived at a definition, there is no certainty that the phenomenon has not changed to such an extent that the definition is no longer valid. For this reason, it is always useful to re-evaluate some familiar notions from time to time and see how they correspond to the reality.

Let us start with the notion of security. For decades, the term "security" has dominated the writings of political scholars. In the Cold War period, on a national level, security was associated with the protection of national borders and non-intervention by other states in a nation's domestic affairs. It was assumed that a state could preserve its security by maintaining a certain level of armament and military preparedness to deal with any possible aggression. National security considerations overrode international security interests. The understanding of national security in military terms was projected into the approach to international—primarily global—security. In practice, national and international security were usually at odds with each other.

In the contemporary world, this traditional understanding of security no longer holds. Today, security has entered a new dimension, and it is no longer possible to ensure the security of one state at the expense of the others. The world has become too interdependent, and a crisis or a conflict in one region immediately triggers reactions all over the globe. Ethnic conflicts in particular easily provoke a chain of related tensions. As a result, national security considerations are now subordinate to international security interests; the latter operate not only in global but often in regional terms as well. A new phenomenon of "neighborhood security" now preoccupies policymakers. Thus, in the contemporary international environment, it is necessary to speak of "common security," which preserves the interests of a single state while providing for its safety through global and regional security arrangements.

Although military and political considerations remain important, security today is no longer limited to these issues. In 1989, following lengthy debate, the United Nations unanimously adopted a new concept of security: "security in all aspects."[1] In other words, security is interpreted today as being comprehensive in nature. In addition to conflict-prevention and disarmament, it includes protection of human rights, promotion of eco-

[1] General Assembly Resolution 44/21 (15 November 1989).

nomic and social development, and preservation of the environment. It is within the context of common security in all its aspects that the answers to national security should be found.

Furthermore, it is important to differentiate clearly between two closely related terms: "security" and "peace." It is noteworthy that in the UN Charter these words are always conjoined. For example, the main purpose of the organization is "to maintain international peace and security."[2] The major reason for the coupling of these two terms was that, at the time the Charter was drafted, the term "security" was not sufficiently defined. In my opinion, security is the notion of an order higher than peace and transcends the simple absence of war to signal the elimination of violence from relations between states. In this connection, I would use the term "positive peace," which means not only refraining from violence but also harmonizing national and global security interests and cooperation between states.

The prerequisite of common security is a system of guarantees. The creation of such a system is perhaps the major challenge now facing the international community. Given the unstable and transitional nature of contemporary international politics, this system will inevitably have a complicated structure, its constituent elements closely intertwined.

With respect to their role in the maintenance of international security, such arrangements may be divided into direct and indirect guarantees. Direct guarantees are measures to eliminate the threat of violence, prevent or peacefully settle international disputes, regulate armaments, and work for disarmament. Indirect guarantees are intended to prevent the recurrence of violence among states and peoples: that is why they seek to create stable social and economic conditions in countries and regions, as well as to democratize international relations.

If we look at the influence of guarantees on international political processes, we can further differentiate between material guarantees, which deal with the reduction of military hardware, and guarantees that have a psychological impact on the international political climate. Of course, the difference between them is relative; any action that reduces armament stockpiles has a positive effect on the political climate. On the other hand, trust and cooperation between states are major prerequisites to practical disarmament. Today, an enriched concept of confidence-building measures is in

[2] Article 1, paragraph 1.

the process of development. In addition to military transparency, this includes a wide variety of measures to promote person-to-person contact.

With regard to application, one might also distinguish between political and legal guarantees. As examples of political guarantees, I would cite the commitments or intentions of states reflected in international political documents, such as the Helsinki Final Act of 1975 or the 1990 Paris Charter of the Conference on Security and Co-operation in Europe (CSCE); the resolutions of the UN General Assembly, which are not obligatory, also belong to this type of guarantee. Legal guarantees are the obligations of states under international treaties and agreements, as well as the decisions of international bodies such as the UN Security Council. Political and legal guarantees support and reinforce each other. Political guarantees, which can also take the form of unilateral actions by states, pave the way for the development of international law; legal guarantees mark the level already achieved by the international community, thus offering states the option to undertake further action.

This notion of security is a complex one, covering a wide range of phenomena. The same can be said of the second notion on our list: multilateralism. The emerging new world order is sometimes called "Pax multilateralis" or "Pax UN"—a system built on the solid foundations of international law, the cornerstone of which is the unique multilateral treaty—the UN Charter. Indeed, multilateral diplomacy is gradually becoming the major tool of international interaction. A convincing example of its importance is the role played today by the UN Security Council. The future of Kuwait, for example, was determined not in Washington, London, Moscow, Paris, or Tokyo, but in New York, at a meeting of the Security Council.

It is worth mentioning that the members of the Security Council—the main decision-making body in the field of international peace and security—are now working on the basis of consensus and demonstrate an unprecedented degree of unity. Even the veto power of the permanent members of the Security Council has acquired a new function. For decades it had a negative impact, blocking the work of the organization; today the veto is a powerful stimulus for compromise. Council members are careful not to provoke others to apply the veto; the existing balance of power is thereby preserved.

The rise of multilateralism in the contemporary, interdependent world is quite a natural process. Only through multilateralism can we hope to find the solution to the numerous global problems which mankind now faces, and only through multilateralism can we safeguard the fragile processes of change and guide them safely into stable, enduring directions. Multilateralism does not mean that all states should necessarily act in concert; within multilateral structures there is room for unilateral, as well as bilateral, action or initiative. A well-known Russian conductor, Evgeniy Mravinsky, once said, "It is keeping up with the general tempo and not slowing it which will preserve the orchestra." This idea applies to international politics as well. It is gratifying that the majority of states have already recognized the full importance of multilateralism.

The contemporary system of multilateral interaction consists of four major layers. At the top is the United Nations, the world's only universal international organization, with its system of seventeen specialized agencies, as well as numerous organs and programs. The United Nations itself—by virtue of its role in international politics—is a very special place. Often described as a microcosm, the United Nations is involved in a wide range of activities in political, economic, and social spheres, and its role in promoting international peace and security is universally recognized. In these turbulent times, the United Nations is the linchpin that holds the world together. However, the United Nations cannot—and was never intended to—solve all the problems of the international community or play the starring role in every political drama; its aim is to initiate, encourage, and harmonize the actions of states in the interests of peace, stability, and the well-being of their people.

The second layer comprises transcontinental arrangements. Some of these, such as the Non-Aligned Movement or the Group of 77, have been in existence for many years. The Organization on Security and Co-operation in Europe (OSCE) has assumed this function. Although the OSCE is technically a regional organization, it incorporates members not only from Europe but also from North America and Asia, and it covers half the Northern Hemisphere. Recently, Japan was granted observer status. This organization stretches from Vladivostok to Vancouver, from Murmansk to Malta, and from Dublin to Dushanbe. The most important feature of the OSCE and other intercontinental organizations is that they are not formed on the basis of economic interests. OSCE members include the most advanced industrial nations of the world as well as developing countries, such as some of the Asian republics of the former Soviet Union. This is a positive trend, because such intercontinental structures may help to overcome the dangerous tendency to divide the world into rich and poor, developed North and underdeveloped South.

The third layer includes the bodies that I would call "classical" regional organizations, such as the Organization of African Unity or the Organization of American States. Today, some of these organizations, in particular those of long standing, are in the process of transition, searching for a new role in the changing international environment. This is true, for example, of NATO, which, although a ready-made mechanism for action, is still searching for its new identity. The idea of a partnership for peace is one guideline for the adaptation of NATO to new realities; implementation of that partnership also requires a well-calculated timetable. No less important, the partnership for peace should be extended not only to the East but also to neutral European countries that are in the same power vacuum. The transformed NATO could become the backbone of pan-European security, closely linked with the OSCE.

The last and fastest-growing layer is the subregional organizations. In Europe in particular during recent years, a large number of new regional and subregional organizations have been established, for example, the Commonwealth of Independent States, the Central European Initiative (also known as the Pentagonal Initiative or the Adriatic-Danube Initiative), the Black Sea Economic Cooperation Organization, and the Council of Baltic States.

Ideally, these four layers should be integrated into a single, interactive structure—a safety net built on division of labor and mutual support. At present we already have some elements of such integration. For example, in May 1993 a framework agreement on cooperation was signed between the United Nations and the then Conference on Security and Co-operation in Europe which, one hopes, will considerably enhance the coordination of the activities of the two organizations.[3] Any crisis in relations among

[3] See Cooperation between the United Nations and the Conference on Security and Cooperation in Europe, General Assembly Resolution 49/13, 49 UN GAOR Supp. (No. 49) at 12, UN doc. A/49/49 (1994).

states should immediately spur the international bodies to action, starting with the subregional organizations, and proceeding, if necessary, up to the Security Council—the only multilateral body empowered, under Chapter VII of the UN Charter, to undertake enforcement action.

In recent years, the United Nations has developed elaborate measures to promote peace. The "four P's"—preventive diplomacy, peacemaking, peacekeeping, and peacebuilding—constitute the major tools of conflict settlement. The United Nations has the knowledge to deal with crises, and it is willing to share it with other international bodies. It should also be kept in mind that the promotion of peace is inseparable from development and democracy. As the secretary-general emphasized in his report on the work of the organization, "Without peace, there can be no development and there can be no democracy. Without development, the basis for democracy will be lacking and societies will tend to fall into conflict. And without democracy, no sustainable development can occur; without such development, peace cannot long be maintained."[4] The joint efforts of international organizations in all these fields should be the major aim of multilateral diplomacy.

The new concept of security and the transformation of multilateral machinery from occasions for ideological confrontation into tools for dynamic action, create the conditions necessary to meet the challenge of our times: to bring about change without disrupting stability. However, realizing these conditions demands a new type of leadership—the collective leadership of the United Nations. All countries, large and small, can contribute substantially to collective leadership; none has a monopoly on quality of foreign policy and diplomacy. The contribution of an individual state to collective diplomacy depends upon its traditions and culture, as well as upon the abilities of the individuals who conduct its foreign affairs.

The conduct of collective leadership is not an easy task. In fact, this is an entirely new phenomenon in the history of international relations. It will require the further democratization of the United Nations' major bodies; it will also require the improvement and refinement of techniques of multilateral interaction. Responsibility should become a catchword for collective leadership in our turbulent times. Last, but not least, collective leader-

[4] "Annual Report on the Work of the Organization," *Official Records of the General Assembly*, 48th Session, 1993, A/48/Supp. 1, para. 11.

ship should be based on moral assumptions different from those that guided the actions of the political leaders of the past.

I would emphasize in particular the moral aspects of collective leadership. Human civilization has reached a stage in its development where moral considerations, as well as ethics in general, can and should become the driving force in international politics. Nothing unites people more than the common understanding of what is evil and what is good, and nothing divides them more than ethical norms of groups or nations that deprive individuals of human dignity and the right to be treated as equals. The importance of morality in social processes is often underestimated; some schools of thought even hold that morality has nothing to do with political reality. World affairs are considered to be the realm of power, coercion, and conflicting national interests; in fact, this has never been true.

From time immemorial, morality has had a considerable impact on foreign policy. The cruelest conquerors acted within the framework of their value system and always justified their deeds by reference to ethical norms. Even during the darkest periods of human history, it was a rare aggressor who admitted that he had attacked his neighbor simply out of greed or any other immoral motive.

The interdependence of the contemporary world stretches beyond the economic and social spheres to include ethics as well. For centuries, mankind has shared some basic moral values. The Ten Commandments in Judaism and Christianity, *Shari'a* in Islam, as well as ethical codes of other religions, contain essentially similar rules of behavior that have eternal value and apply both to individuals and to states. As a result of growing interdependence among nations, the elements of these codes have been incorporated into a number of fundamental international accords. We need to merge ethics and the rule of law in international politics and to create political thinking that will unite rather than divide peoples.

In this connection, I would like to mention the role of Europe. Today, in many spheres, Europe is setting an example for the rest of the world. It adopted the Paris Charter and, at the conferences in Paris, Copenhagen, and Moscow that preceded the charter's adoption, has established the highest standard for the protection of human rights. In fact, the very idea of multilateralism was born in Europe and was first practically implemented with the League of Nations. Let us hope that with due determination

Europe can initiate a new enlightenment that will radically transform the entire international political system.

The new concept of common security in all aspects, the ready-made instrument of its achievement—multilateralism—and world governance through collective, moral political leadership, represent, I believe, the strategic triad that presents a unique opportunity to meet the unprecedented challenges we face today.

The Evolution of the Secretary-General

Brian Urquhart

The fiftieth anniversary of the 1944 Dumbarton Oaks Conversations brings to mind two people in particular who played a very important role in following up on those conversations. The first is Lord Gladwyn, or Gladwyn Jebb as he then was, who was a pillar of the British postwar planning team and one of the world's greatest diplomatic draftsmen. Gladwyn went on to be the executive secretary of the preparatory commission of the United Nations in London and was very largely responsible for setting up the organization on the basis of the UN Charter. In fact, he should rightly be considered as the first secretary-general of the United Nations.

The second is Ralph Bunche. Bunche was a member of the American delegation at Dumbarton Oaks, and he also went on to construct and develop the international organization that was being created in Washington fifty years ago. He was unquestionably the greatest of all international civil servants, and although most famous for his work as mediator in Palestine, he was also a major force in the process of decolonization. He set up the United Nations trusteeship system and was the main drafter of Chapters XI and XII of the Charter on dependent territories and trusteeship. He was also the inventor, father, architect, and first director of UN peacekeeping. Neither of these great international figures has received the recognition that is due their extraordinary achievements.

The title "United Nations" originally referred to nations united in war, a concept much easier to realize than nations uniting in peace. It held no fears, however, for the leaders of the Dumbarton Oaks Conversations fifty years ago. To our timid eyes, the statesmanship and vision that inspired the conversations now seem breathtaking in their scope and spirit. That vision and statesmanship were tempered by hardheaded national diplomacy, which, however, was not allowed to obscure the vision of a new and better world in which nations united both against danger and in pursuit of great common goals. Fifty years ago it was assumed that the new international system would learn from the mistakes of the past and build convincingly for the future.

Unfortunately, the vision of Dumbarton Oaks has been progressively diminished over the years. Sometimes we have even been tempted to retreat from it into what Arthur Schlesinger, Jr. has called the "*sauve qui peut*" world of narrow national interests.[1] Fortunately, so far, this tendency has always been overcome, but throughout the first fifty years of the United Nations it is the secretary-general of the United Nations who has been both the symbol and the keeper of the original vision. The secretary-general has thus been both a catalyst in developing the international framework and a weather vane measuring its success.

Even at the outset there was never any doubt that the secretary-generalship was an important and potentially key institution. In principle, of course, it is easy enough to say that the United Nations needs a strong, imaginative, and independent leader, but in fact it is by no means as easy as that. The United Nations is an intergovernmental organization, and governments have no intention of losing control of it; thus, their attitude to its chief and only elected official is necessarily ambivalent. From the governmental point of view, the secretary-general embodies, if only in the most tentative way, the possibility of something more than international cooperation—even an element of supranationalism. As a result, the secretary-generalship and the performance of its various incumbents have tended often to be controversial in practice. This was particularly true of activist secretaries-general such as Dag Hammarskjöld, and possibly Boutros Boutros-Ghali as well. Perhaps the best description of what governments are looking for in the secretary-general can be found in the anodyne words of Max Finger, a former member of the US delegation to the United Nations, who described it as "excellence within the parameters of political reality."[2] There is nothing straightforward about being secretary-general of the United Nations.

[1] "Bye, Bye Woodrow," *Wall Street Journal*, 27 October 1993.

[2] As cited in Brian Urquhart and Erskine Childers, *A World in Need of Leadership: Tomorrow's United Nations* (Uppsala: Dag Hammarskjöld Foundation, 1990), 18.

Fifty years ago at Dumbarton Oaks the reservations of the Great Powers about the secretary-general's office were already clear. They strongly opposed the direct election of the secretary-general by the General Assembly; they even shot down the idea that the Security Council should recommend the appointment of a secretary-general by a simple majority vote without the application of the veto. The smaller states continued the argument on this, as on other essential matters, at the San Francisco Conference, but the permanent members won. Thus the permanent members have always controlled the appointment of the secretary-general, a responsibility that they have perennially failed to live up to in any serious way.

The descriptions of the job given by the various incumbents also show some ambivalence, born quite frequently of bitter experience. The first secretary-general, Trygve Lie, referred to it as "the most impossible job on this earth."[3] Dag Hammarskjöld said that the secretary-general was rather like "a secular pope, but, more often than not, a pope without a church."[4] U Thant, a courageous and modest man, said that the secretary-generalship was "the most varied, most interesting and most challenging political job on earth," while Kurt Waldheim said that it was "at the same time one of the most fascinating and one of the most frustrating jobs in the world, encompassing as it does the height of human aspiration and the depth of human frailty."[5]

Franklin Roosevelt, who tended to be ahead of his time, thought that the chief executive officer of the United Nations should be called the "moderator," and indeed that would have conveyed the essence of the secretary-general's most important function. My compatriots, the British, however, pointed out that there was already a moderator of the Church of Scotland and that, improbable as it now seems, there would be confusion. The more prosaic title of secretary-general was therefore chosen.

[3] Trygve Lie's welcome to Dag Hammarskjöld, Idlewild Airport, New York, 9 April 1953. Brian Urquhart, *Hammarskjöld* (New York: Alfred A. Knopf, 1972), 15.

[4] Urquhart, *Hammarskjöld,* 51.

[5] U Thant, speech at luncheon of the Memorial Scholarship Fund of the United Nations Correspondents Association, 16 September 1971, UN press release SG/SM/1531; Kurt Waldheim, statement to the General Assembly on his reelection, 8 December 1976, UN doc. A/31/PV.93.

The founders of the United Nations were discreetly vague about the scope and nature of the secretary-general's work, and it is perhaps this fact above all others that has allowed the secretary-generalship to develop and to grow more than any other United Nations organ. Despite Franklin Roosevelt's vision of the job, the primary task of the secretary-general was originally to be the chief administrative officer of the organization, with rather limited obligations to carry out the decisions of the main organs of the United Nations. Only Article 99 of the Charter opens the door to independent political action—and it doesn't open it much. Under Article 99 the secretary-general "may bring to the attention of the Security Council any matter which in his opinion may threaten the maintenance of international peace and security." If the secretary-general has any independent political role under the Charter, this article is its basis.

When it came to appointing the first secretary-general, governments were extraordinarily vague as to what they were looking for. It certainly never seems to have occurred to anyone that the secretary-general could possibly be a woman. In September 1945 we find Adlai Stevenson telling Secretary of State Edward R. Stettinius, Jr., "We favor choice of an outstandingly qualified individual, preferably a figure who has attained some international position and preferably a national of a small or middle power."[6] This is not exactly overwhelming as a job description. In late December 1945, when the appointment of the first secretary-general was imminent, the State Department mused, "A more common acceptance of the qualifications required for the secretary-general would be helpful in arriving at a decision."[7]

They would have no such luck. It soon became brutally clear, after some eminent names—Dwight Eisenhower, Anthony Eden, Lester Pearson—had been bandied about and turned down, that the secretary-general's appointment would be a cynically political decision. I first became aware of this when the first General Assembly was considering nominations for the first secretary-general. At that time, among many other duties, I ran the speakers list in the General Assembly, and Mr. Stettinius came up to my table to ask me to point out Trygve Lie, who was then

[6] US Department of State archives, as cited in Urquhart and Childers, *World in Need of Leadership,* 16.

[7] Ibid.

foreign minister of Norway. I identified the large figure of Mr. Lie for Stettinius, who then went up to the rostrum and referred to Lie as "a statesman known to us all," "a household word," a "name famous among the heroes of World War II" and similar epithets. The United Nations got Trygve Lie, who described himself as "a labor lawyer from Norway." I shall come back to the irresponsible nature of the appointment process later on.

The secretary-generalship is theoretically an impossible job. Quite apart from unreal expectations and lack of any real power and the contrary attitudes of governments, it includes an unmanageable number of major functions. These are

- managing the Secretariat and living on a shoestring budget, much of which is not paid up;
- coordinating the so-called UN system of specialized agencies and major programs, a task which presents problems rather like those that King John of England had with the feudal barons;
- representing the United Nations worldwide;
- maintaining a watch on major developments of all kinds;
- carrying out the decisions of the Security Council and other organs of the United Nations;
- running peacekeeping and other highly sensitive operations;
- being the world's chief "honest broker" engaged in endless missions of good offices and quiet diplomacy all over the world;
- providing good offices in human rights and humanitarian situations;
- generating ideas and strategies on global problems;
- and, one perhaps might add, being the world's number one fig leaf and scapegoat.

The secretary-general is a civil servant with 185 masters at this time but is also expected to be a leader. As U Thant put it, "The Secretary-General's activity will usually seem to some governments too much, and to others too little. He must thread his way through the jungle of conflicting national policies with the Charter as his compass, and, if he is lucky, with a directive from one of the main deliberative organs as his guide."[8]

The main factors in the development of the secretary-generalship have been the personalities of the incumbents and the political climate in which they worked. The secretary-general is now recognized as the world's num-

[8] U Thant, speech to the UN Correspondents Association, 16 September 1971.

ber one "honest broker," but this was not originally the case. In 1946 governments were extraordinarily sensitive about any pretension to political activity by the secretary-general. The British in particular constantly referred to the almost obsessive discretion of Sir Eric Drummond, the British secretary-general of the League of Nations, who had never made a public statement or addressed a public meeting of the league during his entire career as secretary-general.

The Cold War meant that it was often difficult for the secretary-general to avoid a collision with one of the superpowers when the superpowers disagreed on what action should be taken. This was true of Trygve Lie and the United Nations operation in Korea, and, later, of Dag Hammarskjöld in the Congo. But the Cold War also made a nonpartisan third party indispensable if total paralysis in the Security Council was to be avoided.

Acting, as often, without checking the facts, the Security Council appointed Dag Hammarskjöld to succeed Lie under the delightful misapprehension that Hammarskjöld was a nonpolitical technocrat. Hammarskjöld soon showed the value of the office even on Cold War issues. His first great triumph was the release of seventeen United States airmen held by the Chinese as prisoners of the Korean War. He went on to develop the secretary-general's negotiating possibilities as well as fielding peacekeeping forces, of which the first experiment was in the Suez Crisis of 1956. Thus Hammarskjöld pioneered a new role for the secretary-general as crisis manager and director of active peace operations.

Hammarskjöld eventually paid a heavy price for his success, which tended to alienate one or other of the permanent members of the Security Council. He had already run up against the United States over Guatemala and against the French and the British over Suez, and in the Congo he infuriated both the French and the Soviets. He finally alienated de Gaulle for good by his actions when the French reoccupied Bizerte in Tunisia. Hammarskjöld pushed the secretary-generalship and the international civil service very far toward becoming an active independent team for peace. In fighting to preserve the independence and integrity of the secretariat he suffered many attacks in his final years.

Hammarskjöld set a very high standard by the importance he attached to what he called "working on the edge of human society" for a "creative evolution" of human institutions.[9] His idea was to build pragmatically a

[9] Address to the University of Chicago Law School, 1 May 1960, UN doc. S/G 910.

reliable and just world order by making precedents and case law, thus gradually transforming the United Nations from an institutional mechanism into a constitutional instrument and system for dealing with the world's problems. This was a very ambitious goal indeed, but it is worth raising our eyes from time to time to contemplate it.

Dag Hammarskjöld's death in the Congo left the United Nations split down the middle. U Thant, his successor, picked up the pieces and reunited the organization. Of all the secretaries-general, he is the one who has been most unjustly forgotten. It is perhaps not too surprising, since he had a moral view of his office and responsibilities. He was a person of great honesty and courage, but he was not always taken too seriously. He played an important role in resolving the Cuban Missile Crisis, he was instrumental in securing a cease-fire in the war between India and Pakistan in 1965, and on his own responsibility he made a spirited effort to bring the Vietnam War to an end. The withdrawal of the UN Emergency Force (UNEF I) in the Middle East and the subsequent Six-Day War overshadowed everything else in his stewardship. He served as a useful scapegoat for that occasion, although he was the only person who went to Cairo and tried to persuade Gamal Abdel Nasser to reconsider his disastrous course.

U Thant's successor, Kurt Waldheim, and his rival Max Jakobson of Finland, were the first candidates to campaign actively for the office, a disastrous precedent which has been followed ever since. Waldheim was not an inspiring leader or an original thinker, but he held the fort during the tumultuous 1970s. He reestablished peacekeeping as an indispensable international technique after the 1967 UNEF disaster. After he left, he was discovered to have falsified his war record and became the subject of almost universal opprobrium in the West. It would have been perfectly possible to have established what his war record was before he was appointed to the job, but nobody bothered. It is important to remember, in the context of the way the secretary-general is appointed, that had it not been for China, Kurt Waldheim would have won a third term with the active support of the United States and the United Kingdom.

Waldheim's successor, Javier Perez de Cuellar, was a quiet and honest diplomat and probably as good a person as any to be secretary-general during the transition from the Cold War to the uncertainties we are now enjoying. He kept on good terms with all governments and was a popular but not, perhaps, a striking international figure. He presided with great skill over the short-lived and illusory "renaissance" of the United Nations in the early 1990s. Perez de Cuellar's successor, Boutros-Ghali, inherited the difficult transition to the post-Cold War world.

It is worth noting that none of the secretaries-general except Dag Hammarskjöld was a manager and administrator, nor did any of them except Hammarskjöld show much interest in the economic and social side of the United Nations, which accounts for some eighty percent of the organization's activity in terms of staff and budget. But, overall, it is possible to say that given the total lack of any serious selection process, the United Nations has been relatively lucky with its secretaries-general.

It remains to be seen whether anyone has any intention of improving the way the secretary-general is appointed. The current process would be rejected as a joke by any serious organization in the private sector. At the very minimum, the Security Council and the General Assembly should formulate some description of what they are looking for and adopt a proper search process to identify the best men and women in the world for the job. The veto should not apply to the appointment, and by the same token the ban on candidates from the permanent members might be lifted. The temptation to run for reelection has never improved the performance of the people who have been secretary-general. A single seven-year term would allow any serious person enough time to carry out their program without being distracted by the desire to be reelected.

Boutros Boutros-Ghali was unquestionably an activist secretary-general. He had a number of problems quite apart from his personal approach to the job. In the post-Cold War world the secretary-general as political intermediary is less essential than he used to be. As the operational director of the United Nations he has a huge and expanding task, but dwindling resources. The financial base of the United Nations is more insecure than ever, with some governments—especially the United States—far behind in their payments. As someone who came to office with the announced intention of reorganizing the United Nations, Boutros-Ghali had to try to reorganize a machine that was going at full speed down the open highway.

Boutros-Ghali had another problem. His authority was increasingly questioned, especially as regards the command and control of United Nations operations. Above all, he had to face a schizophrenic perception of the United Nation's role. The public and the media increasingly regard it as the police-and-rescue service of a world community, while governments do not recognize this role and are reluctant to give it the resources and infrastructure the organization needs for such purposes.

The original spirit of international solidarity in the United Nations has been very much weakened in recent years. There is an increasing tendency to look for coalitions of the like-minded in difficult situations and to de-emphasize the UN role. This does not mean that the United Nations will not be just as much, or more, in demand than ever when governments desperately need a dumping ground for an urgent but unwelcome problem.

There is considerable suspicion at the moment both of the Security Council in its elitist post-Cold War role and, as always, of an activist secretary-general. Although the "world community" scarcely exists in reality, the public and media expect the United Nations to act as its police-and-rescue service. In the current circumstances this means that the United Nations deals less with conflicts between states, for which it was set up, and more with civil and ethnic conflicts within states, for which it was very definitely not designed. All in all, the secretary-general is busier than ever and perhaps lonelier than ever; he is trying to lead an international organization in a period of resurgent nationalism, of growing distrust of international institutions, and of diminishing support from governments.

The question, however, remains: Will the institutions of a working world community be developed before it is too late? Or are we to continue with the *ad hoc* sheriff's posse approach, which is usually too late and almost always inefficient and expensive? The secretary-general has a unique responsibility in the "creative evolution" of which Dag Hammarskjöld spoke. The secretary-general is the executive head of the world organization, appointed in the name of all governments. He is the head of the world's international civil service. He, or, in the future I hope, she, is a vital symbol and a vital element in the development of the global society based on law that is probably our only long-term hope and our only alternative to a progressive decline into chaos.

Douglas J. Bennet, assistant secretary of state for International Organization Affairs, delivers the keynote address for the "Dumbarton Oaks Conference, 1944–1994" in the Loy Henderson Conference Room at the Department of State, 5 May 1994. (photo: Elisa Komins)

Neil L. Rudenstine, president of Harvard University, opens the conference at Dumbarton Oaks on 6 May 1994 with the same gavel—made of wood from the U.S.S. *Constitution*—used to officially convene the 1944 Dumbarton Oaks Conversations. (photo: Elisa Komins)

Prior to delivering his paper, "The Developing Role of the Secretary-General," Sir Brian Urquhart (*left*), a former UN under secretary-general, speaks with Angeliki E. Laiou, director of Dumbarton Oaks and a Harvard professor of history, and Ernest R. May, a professor at the John F. Kennedy School of Government at Harvard. (photo: Elisa Komins)

Questions from the audience are taken by the panel for International Institutions and International Security. Seated are (*left to right*) Lori F. Damrosch, professor of law at Columbia University; Stanley Hoffmann, professor at the Center for European Studies at Harvard University; and Indar Jit Rikhye, senior research associate at the United States Institute of Peace.
(photo: Elisa Komins)

Mahbub ul Haq, special adviser to the UN Development Programme administrator, addresses conference attendees as part of the panel for Issues of Economic Development and the Environment. (photo: Elisa Komins)

Joseph S. Nye, Jr., chairman of the National Intelligence Council, moderates a roundtable discussion, The Future: Capabilities and Limitations of International Institutions and Organizations. Seated are (*left to right*) Tom Farer, professor at the Washington College of Law and School of International Service, American University; Nancy Landon Kassebaum, US senator, R–Kansas; Peter Leuprecht, deputy secretary-general for the Council of Europe; Mario Ojeda-Gómez, president of El Colegio de México; Albrecht G. Muth, personal representative for Vladimir Petrovsky, director-general of the UN Geneva Office; and Paul Sarbanes, US senator, D–Maryland. (photo: Elisa Komins)

Opening session of the Dumbarton Oaks Conversations, held in the Music Room at Dumbarton Oaks, beginning 21 August 1944. Seated at the speaker's table at the far end of the room are (*left to right*) Sir Alexander Cadogan, chairman of the British delegation; Earl of Halifax, British ambassador to the United States; Cordell Hull, US secretary of state; Andrei A. Gromyko, Soviet ambassador to the United States and chairman of the Soviet delegation; Edward R. Stettinius, Jr., US under secretary of state and chairman of the US delegation. (photo: Courtesy of the National Archives, Washington, D.C.)

Some of the delegates hold an informal discussion in the study at Dumbarton Oaks. Seated are (*left to right*) Peter Loxley, private secretary to Sir Alexander Cadogan; Sir Alexander Cadogan, chairman of the British delegation; Edward R. Stettinius, Jr., US under secretary of state and chairman of the US delegation; Andrei A. Gromyko, Soviet ambassador to the United States and chairman of the Soviet delegation; Arkadii A. Sobolev, minister-counselor of the Soviet embassy in London; Valentin M. Berezhkov, counselor at the Soviet Foreign Ministry. Standing are (*left to right*) James Clement Dunn, director of the Office of European Affairs, and Leo Pasvolsky, special assistant to the US secretary of state and executive director of the Post-War Programs Committee. (photo: Courtesy of the National Archives, Washington, D.C.)

Delegations representing the United States, Great Britain, and the Soviet Union assemble for a group photograph on the north lawn of Dumbarton Oaks. (photo: Courtesy of the National Archives, Washington, D.C.)

(*standing*) Edward R. Stettinius, Jr., US under secretary of state and chairman of the US delegation, addresses reporters in the Music Room at Dumbarton Oaks, informing them that the United States, Great Britain, and the Soviet Union had reached a general agreement concerning the structure and goals of an international organization for peace and security. (photo: Courtesy of the National Archives, Washington, D.C.)

(*left to right*) V. K. Wellington Koo, chairman of the Chinese delegation, Edward R. Stettinius, Jr., US under secretary of state and chairman of the US delegation, and Sir Alexander Cadogan, chairman of the British delegation, discuss matters during the second phase of the conversations, which opened on 29 September 1944 at Dumbarton Oaks. (photo: Courtesy of the National Archives, Washington, D.C.)

Lessons of the Postwar Experience in Europe

Karl Kaiser

The year 1994 provides a particularly fruitful vantage point from which to review half a century of world politics and the impact of the ideas discussed at Dumbarton Oaks fifty years ago. The international politics of the postwar period is now undergoing profound change. The Cold War era has come to an end and a new era has begun. How successfully did the ideas developed at Dumbarton Oaks operate during the East-West conflict, where did they fail, and what do the changes toward a new era mean for the Dumbarton Oaks concept of a United Nations?

This analysis starts from the central proposition that the concept of the United Nations that was formulated at Dumbarton Oaks had a marginal impact in the Northern Hemisphere—what was later called the First and the Second Worlds—whereas its impact on the Southern Hemisphere—the Third World—was more significant.

During the East-West conflict, the antagonism between the two camps led by the United States and the Soviet Union soon paralyzed the Security Council and, thereby, the crucial function of the United Nations in the field of peace and security. The conflicts of power and of ideology during the Cold War years rendered the United Nations ineffective in dealing with problems of aggression, of freedom, and of fighting authoritarian forces (to use the terminology of the Truman Doctrine). The disagreements, for example, on possible peace settlements and the future of Germany or of Europe were profound. Wherever the two camps, and particularly the two leading powers, were directly involved, it turned out to be impossible to come to any major agreement.

It was not the collective security of the Dumbarton Oaks and San Francisco conferences that secured international peace. Instead, peace was maintained first, through a network of alliances built up around the world

(NATO being the most important) and, second, by the system of nuclear deterrence. Since war was no longer conceivable as a continuation of policy by other means, deterrence made war unwageable. The key concept of the era of nuclear deterrence was stability, and as the destructive power of the nuclear arsenals grew, stability became both more crucial and more encompassing. This very system of deterrence carried within it the seeds of change, however, because it forced the participating powers to cooperate in order to prevent a nuclear war, which would certainly have meant self-annihilation and possibly the annihilation of all mankind. Cooperation among the antagonists developed from there, profoundly changing the nature of the East-West system and, eventually, of global politics.

Arms control thus emerged as a central arena of relations in the Northern Hemisphere. In this process the role of the United Nations was insignificant. The United States, supported by its allies, on the one hand, and the Soviet Union, assisted occasionally by its satellites, on the other, were the major players. The parties to the East-West conflict moved things ahead. The United Nations was sometimes useful in providing concepts or a framework in which to conduct negotiations, but the moving forces were the Great Powers themselves. The first important agreements—the Test Ban, the Hotline, SALT I, SALT II, even the Non-Proliferation Treaty—were shaped by them.

The first genuine disarmament agreement after World War II, the INF Treaty of 1987, was concluded between the United States and the Soviet Union. The United Nations was a framework for debate and articulation of positions but not for action. The dynamics of change that in the end brought down the Cold War system owed very little, if anything, to the United Nations. The forces of change instead came from within the system that had emerged in the Northern Hemisphere. Change in the West was generated by the growing practice of arms control. The process included nuclear learning, détente policy (which started in particular after the NATO alliance had formulated a new strategy in the Harmel exercise of 1967), Germany's new *Ostpolitik* and *Deutschlandpolitik*, and the ensuing multilateral phase of the Conference on Security and Co-operation in Europe, driven by the Europeans and, if not encouraged, then at least tolerated by the Nixon administration. These developments led to change. They opened borders, created new contacts, transformed old opinions, and, in the end, truly brought down the Communist system. The forces of change within the East itself, however, were also significant. The irresistible urge for freedom and, in particular, the utter social and economic failure of Communism eroded the totalitarian system. To be sure, East and West occasionally cooperated within the United Nations during this period, but usually on issues regarding the Third World. With respect to controversies between East and West, the United Nations provided a forum for what Inis Claude called a "Grand Debate Approach to Peace,"[1] where the two sides sought support for their policies in the debates of the General Assembly.

It was therefore not within the United Nations but within the East-West system that peace was secured in the Northern Hemisphere. Throughout this period, however, a historic change was taking place within the East-West system that would have corresponded to the visions of some (if not all) of the planners who gathered at Dumbarton Oaks fifty years ago, visions that the United Nations had failed to implement during its early decades. The change was, indeed, profound: As a consequence of continued cooperation among Western states, a constellation of interests was created in which the use of force was reliably excluded as a means of resolving conflict between them. Cooperation also promoted integration, delegation of certain state powers, transnational links, and growing interdependence, all of which culminated in the European Community and the European Union. Inter-state relations within the NATO alliance (with the possible exception of the Greek-Turkish relationship) and, indeed, among member states of the Organization for Economic Co-operation and Development (OECD) are essentially peaceful; war between its members is prohibited.

By contrast, the role of the United Nations in the Southern Hemisphere during the Cold War was quite different; there, it had a significant impact. To be sure, in certain conflicts, even where the Great Powers confronted each other directly (as they did during the Vietnam War), they could not come to an agreement, nor did the United Nations have an impact. Sometimes the Great Powers agreed initially and then disagreed. The UN Congo operation started with Soviet approval, but then continued without it. During this period an enormous amount of innovation took place within the United Nations; the organization developed preven-

[1] Inis Claude, *Swords into Plowshares: The Problems and Progress of International Organization* (New York: Random House, 1964), 304 ff.

tive diplomacy, notably through peacekeeping, in order to prevent Great Power involvement in regional conflicts. This innovation had its most significant impact after the Cold War came to an end, as the spectacular expansion of UN peacekeeping activities demonstrates. An instrument originally developed to prevent conflict between East and West turned out to be a most effective and sought-for vehicle in a world of multiple conflicts at the sub-state level.

The United Nations helped to bring about an end to hostilities in various conflicts—Palestine, Kashmir, the Middle East, Korea, Cyprus—though its intervention did not settle the underlying issues. Success on human rights issues has been especially limited. Except for the codification of human rights and the prolonged struggle to bring down apartheid, the United Nations' impact has been marginal. Even in its efforts against apartheid, however, the United Nations undermined its credibility with a double standard, criticizing South Africa's policy while remaining silent on incidents of genocide elsewhere and on the massive repression of human rights in the Soviet bloc.

As far as the Southern Hemisphere is concerned, the most significant impact of the United Nations has been to accelerate decolonization, a development that essentially changed the structure of world politics and, indeed, the structure of the United Nations itself. The United Nations has also succeeded in turning development into the central issue of the UN system, thereby assisting the Southern Hemisphere in creating new organizations, mobilizing the transfer of funds and enlisting public understanding and support for the problems of the Third World in developing democracies.

Surely, positive change with regard to the ideas developed at Dumbarton Oaks and in San Francisco is conspicuous today. The end of the East-West conflict removed the main obstacle to common action and restored the Security Council as the central organ for peace and security. After 1990, the council began to exercise the functions envisioned for it by the original planners: It mandated the use of force to liberate occupied Kuwait and, for the first time, acted as the supreme organ to punish violation of rules of non-proliferation under the International Atomic Energy Agency by imposing nuclear and chemical disarmament on Iraq. For the first time, the Security Council, and thereby the United Nations, intervened in domestic affairs of a country to protect minorities—the Kurds and the Shiites. In

Somalia, it intervened to stop anarchy, even though the outcome suggests failure. In the former Yugoslavia, the Security Council has been able to take action in numerous ways under Chapter VII. Whatever its deficiencies, the United Nations is at last available to intervene to uphold the principles of the Charter. On many recent occasions the Great Powers have come to agreement. (Whether they will continue to agree as crises develop is an open question.) Moreover, for the first time regional organizations—NATO, for example—are available to legitimately serve the purposes of the United Nations.

With the end of the Cold War, new problems have arisen and old ones have been aggravated, creating new and demanding challenges for the UN system. First, ancient conflicts and hatreds suppressed for decades, indeed centuries, have returned, notably in the Balkans and the Caucasus. Second, the peace that had been secured throughout the postwar period in the Northern Hemisphere has broken down in Eastern and Southeastern Europe. Civil war, inter-state war, ethnic and religious conflict, and, indeed, genocidal actions have come back to haunt Europe. Third, political authority and governability are declining, not only in the Third World, but also in formerly socialist states, including Russia. These regions and their governments are no longer viable partners in global policy because they lack authority and resources. Fourth, migration is becoming an issue of growing importance in global politics. Finally, poverty and ecological crises continue to plague the global system.

All of these problems have to be considered in the context of the persistent heritage of the Cold War, which makes them more difficult to resolve. I would like to mention three important factors. First, arsenals piled up during the four decades of the Cold War are now easily available and are flooding into a world divided by conflict. Second, the proliferation of nuclear and chemical weapons will carry over as a major issue in this new era. The initial five nuclear states have expanded to eight (not counting South Africa, which was a nuclear state and subsequently disarmed its arsenal, and North Korea, which has renounced its nuclear weapons program but may resume it if circumstances change). Nuclear proliferation is a particularly burning issue if one considers the potential risks of its spillover into other conflicts. These problems are connected to a third heritage of the Cold War—the proliferation of missile technology, which removes the protection of distance once and for all.

All of these factors exist in an environment characterized by growing global interdependence and by mutual vulnerability. Consequently, when damage occurs it spreads throughout the system and beyond borders. Global politics is more interconnected than ever, and distance no longer provides any protection.

While the ideas of those who assembled at Dumbarton Oaks in 1944 had only a marginal impact on international politics in the Northern Hemisphere, they had a profound impact in shaping politics during the Cold War in the South. It was in the South that the original system of ideas was kept alive and innovation took place. They helped to prevent some conflicts, to end others, and to support self-determination and development. After the Cold War, with grave new challenges arising both to world peace and to human rights, the United Nations is more necessary than ever and will, I hope, be able to act through its institutions.

In facing this task, the United Nations will hopefully be assisted by a force that the planners assembled at Dumbarton Oaks could not have foreseen, namely, the vast group of states assembled in the enlarging European Union, in NATO, and in the OECD. Amidst the revival of bloody wars, genocide, and anarchy that we are witnessing, this community of nations has reliably excluded the use of force as a means to resolve their conflicts. The impact of this historical change may well create a constellation of interests in the coming era that will insure that we do not experience another pause of forty-five years until the United Nations has a chance to work along the lines the planners drew at Dumbarton Oaks fifty years ago.

A Hope That Still Might Come True

Henry Trofimenko

In August 1946, after graduating from high school, I enrolled in the Moscow State Institute of International Relations to study international law. The new institute and its even newer law department were specially established by the Politburo to provide cadres for the postwar expansion of Soviet diplomacy. One reason for this expansion was the creation of the United Nations, which had the Soviet Union as one of its founders.

Somehow, expectations that the Soviet government and its foreign office would need large numbers of international lawyers never materialized. In a totalitarian and perforce lawless state, the main criterion for job selection was unquestionable obedience to superiors, not prowess in some specific branch of political or legal science. Nonetheless, studying international law was enjoyable because we often had to tackle hot political issues, which we all liked. One of the advantages to studying in this institute was that even students could have access to foreign papers such as the *New York Times,* quite an unusual thing for a Russian university at that time.

One of the prominent subjects in the study of international law was the newly created United Nations—its legal status, its functions, and its mode of operations. Some of our professors, among them, Sergei Krylov and Vladimir Durdenevsky, participated very closely in the drafting of the UN Charter (Krylov was a member of the Soviet delegation to the Dumbarton Oaks Conversations), and they supplied us with a great deal of inside information on the process of negotiating the birth of the organization. They explained to us that the key principle of UN operations was the unanimity of the five permanent members of the UN Security Council—the main body responsible for UN peacekeeping operations. They invariably stressed that the unanimity principle had been proposed by President Franklin Roosevelt and that the role of the Soviet delegations at Dumbarton

Oaks and, later, in San Francisco was to support this key principle staunchly and to energetically prevent it from being diluted or undermined by the enemies of the Great Powers' unanimity.

Later on, when, as an academic, I acquainted myself more thoroughly with the problems of the United Nations, I understood that, while defending the unanimity principle, the Soviet government interpreted it in absolute terms as a guarantee that the principle would prohibit other nations from disputing the Soviet Union's international activities, much less censuring or restraining them through the mechanism of the United Nations. Nevertheless, the principle, as it is embedded in the Charter, is generally sound. If the UN Charter permitted the Security Council to go after one of the Great Powers, such actions would only exacerbate any conflict in which one of the Big Five was involved.

A wave of indignation arose in the United States in 1994 because the secretary-general of the United Nations tried to make limited use of US combat planes over Bosnia without notifying the White House in advance (despite the fact that the planes had already been transferred by the United States to UN operational control). Opponents wondered why the United States had relinquished control over its military forces. One need not be very imaginative to envision the reaction of the American public had the UN Security Council tried to restrain a US military action. The principle of unanimity, then, has been advantageous not only for the Soviet Union, as was claimed in the West in the 1950s and 1960s, but for every permanent member of the Security Council as well, and for the United Nations in general.

One of the first to sympathize with the Soviet position with respect to the unanimity principle and to grasp all its far-flung implications was Field Marshal Jan Christiaan Smuts, the prime minister of the Union of South Africa. In a letter to Winston Churchill, relayed to President Roosevelt at the end of the Dumbarton Oaks Conversations, Smuts emphasized that the principle involved the "honour and standing of Russia amongst her allies." He continued:

> [Russia] asks whether she is trusted and treated as an equal or is still an outlaw and Pariah. . . . On merits there is much to be said for unanimity amongst the Great Powers. . . . If Russia proves impossible the World Organization may have to act but the blame will be hers. At the worst

> the principle of unanimity will only have the effect of a veto, of preventing action where it may be wise or even necessary. It will be negative and slow down action but it will also make it impossible for Russia to embark on activities disapproved by the United Kingdom and United States. Where the people are drunk with newly-won power, it may not be so bad a thing to have a brake like unanimity.[1]

The Soviet foreign minister, Andrei Gromyko, who was Moscow's ambassador to the United States at the time and the head of the Soviet delegation at the Dumbarton Oaks Conversations, fought like a lion for inclusion of the unanimity principle in the UN Charter. Reasoning that it is better to avoid action ten times than to make one *faux pas,* Gromyko was an ideal errand boy for Joseph Stalin. There were many demands to press with regard to the composition and workings of the United Nations, though most of them were negotiable. One such demand was Moscow's insistence that all sixteen Soviet national republics be made members of the United Nations in their own right. To facilitate this, the Soviet parliament adopted a special law in February 1944 that granted Soviet constituent republics the right to conduct independent diplomatic relations and to enter into legally binding agreements with foreign countries. In retrospect, this action seems like the first step in the long process that led to the final demise of the Soviet Union, though it was billed at the time by Vyacheslav Molotov, the Soviet foreign minister, as a great triumph of Leninist/Stalinist national policy. This gimmick did not work and instead infuriated Roosevelt. To prevent a burst of outrage by the American public, he kept Stalin's request top secret. Finally Roosevelt acquiesced to the proposal that additional seats in the United Nations be reserved exclusively for Ukraine and Byelorussia. Stalin persuaded Roosevelt that these two Soviet republics ought to have separate seats because of their outstanding contribution to the defeat of Germany in World War II.

It is significant that it never dawned on Stalin to ask for a seat for Russia, the republic that made the most decisive contribution to the Soviet Union's war effort. Why did he shun Russia? Because there was never in his mind any distinction between Russia and the Soviet Union itself. If

[1] US Department of State, *Foreign Relations of the United States: Diplomatic Papers, 1944,* 2 vols. (Washington, D.C.: Government Printing Office, 1966), 1:837–38.

only two of the Soviet republics were to have separate seats in the United Nations then Russia would not be among them since the Soviet Union's seat was Russian.

To what extent was Stalin ready to cooperate with the West in building a postwar global order? Did he really want to work hand in glove with the United States, the United Kingdom, France, and all other countries in making the world safe, if not for democracy, then at least from a new war? Stalin, for all his nastiness, scheming, and beastliness with regard to his own people, was serious about cooperation. War did not figure in his plans, and, if left unharassed in Eastern Europe, he was quite prepared to police the world together with the United States, conveniently picking up in the process some neglected chunks of land through UN trusteeship and other arrangements.

The Western leaders themselves ratified at Yalta and Potsdam a much greater expansion of Soviet territory than Stalin managed to obtain in his 1939 pact with Adolph Hitler. The non-recognition by Washington of Stalin's annexation of the Baltic states was a *pro-forma* gesture that did not change the real situation a jot. In reality, as Henry Kissinger argues, President Roosevelt had already indicated at the Tehran conference that he would not press Stalin on the question of the Baltics. If Soviet armies occupied the Baltic states, he said, neither the United States nor Great Britain would "turn her out."[2]

In addition to those concessions, it was a great achievement for Stalin, shunned for so long by Western leaders as an outlaw, to be finally accepted as a peer in the global gentlemen's club. He was quite comfortable with Roosevelt's idea that the Soviet Union ought to be one of the "Four Policemen" of the world. Averell Harriman describes in his memoirs how, during a meeting with Churchill and Stalin in August 1942, the British leader painted a rosy picture of the relationship between the three Great Powers. Churchill recalled, writes Harriman, "that in 1938, before Munich, he had drawn up a plan for a League of the Three Great Democracies, as he tactfully described them for Stalin's benefit: Great Britain, the United States and the Soviet Union. Between them they could have stopped the future drift to war, as there were no antagonistic interests to divide them. Stalin

[2] Henry Kissinger, *Diplomacy* (New York: Simon and Schuster, 1994), 411.

said that he always had hoped for some development of this nature but it proved impossible with Neville Chamberlain in Downing Street."[3]

The wily Churchill was evidently trying to entice Stalin with the "union of democracies" in order to sweeten the bitter pill that the second front would not be opened in 1942, but Stalin, I am sure, took it quite seriously. He did not want the Soviet Union, the main contributor to the defeat of Germany, to get into a situation similar to the one the United States faced after World War I, when Republicans in the US Senate prevented the victorious country from joining its own creation—the League of Nations, the precursor of the United Nations. Moreover, Stalin knew that he held the trump card; without the newly vigorous and mighty Soviet Union, the United Nations would be nothing but the debating club that the League of Nations became without the United States. In his desire to accommodate his main war-time allies, Stalin thus yielded to the United States and Britain on almost all the points of contention in connection with the structure of the United Nations. The one point on which he would not compromise was the full and unconditional implementation of the unanimity principle.

With the rise of Cold War passions, however, the unanimity principle degenerated into a negative veto, used mainly by the Soviet Union and the United States. Frequent use of the veto paralyzed the Security Council until the end of the 1980s, and, because of the bipolar division of the world, the United Nations became severely incapacitated. It required a revolution in the Soviet Union for the global role of the United Nations, as envisaged by the great democrat Franklin Roosevelt, to be revived. The effectiveness of some recent UN peacekeeping operations is based on a new concord of the five permanent members of its Security Council. This unanimity, as well as the role of the United Nations as a global peacekeeper, is tested daily—by rising nationalism, by radical extremism, by the divergent economic and political interests of national and ethnic groupings, and by suicidal clan warfare.

Whether the United Nations will eventually live up to the expectations of its founding fathers again depends essentially on the extent of

[3] William Averell Harriman, *Special Envoy to Churchill and Stalin, 1941–1946* (New York: Random House, 1975), 135.

cooperation among the Big Five or, more to the point, the "Big Nine"—the union of the Big Five and the G-7 countries. Bosnia and North Korea are daily reminders of the vital importance of the unanimity principle. The fifty-year experience of the United Nations shows that the organization cannot productively function as a peacemaking and peacekeeping body without strict observance and application of this principle.

As for Russia today, even the Great Victory itself seems to have vanished for many Russians. The nationalistic appeal of aggressive demagogues seems attractive to many in Russia and other former Soviet republics. To take advantage of that appeal, even mainstream politicians in Russia are now trying to demonstrate that they are also true nationalists. Therein lies a great danger to political relations between Russia and the United States and, by implication, to world peace.

Another danger is the residual Cold War mentality that divides the world into "ours" and "theirs." There are, however, more independent players now on what might be called the global nuclear soccer field. Hope for the world today lies not in individual master passes but in team play under the auspices of the United Nations.

Big Power Assurance of Peace Versus the Principle of Equality among All Nations

Zi Zhongyun

Sitting at the UN General Assembly are representatives from 185 nations with one vote for each regardless of the nation's size, population, or strength. Any suggestion that they should not be equal and that smaller countries should have less say would certainly trigger a furor of protest, especially among the developing countries, given the stipulation in the UN Charter that "the Organization is based on the principle of the sovereign equality of all its members."

However, to claim that the founding of the United Nations was based on the principle of "equality among all nations" as it is understood today would be quite misleading. What was in the mind of the organization's founders was clearly the idea of the assurance of peace by the big powers after the war. The smaller nations were to have very little say in the matter. In fact, it was the Big Three—the United States, the United Kingdom, and the Soviet Union—that decided among themselves the structure and working procedure of the potential international organization. Who would be qualified to join them and at what stage was also their decision.

To put it bluntly, China's status as one of the Big Four was the result of President Franklin Roosevelt's insistence, against the opposition of both Winston Churchill and Joseph Stalin. The recognition of France as the fifth big power was due partly to Churchill's persistent pleading and partly to necessity, both of which prevailed over Stalin's scorn for France and Roosevelt's resentment of General Charles de Gaulle. It would be wrong, however, to conclude that the big power status of China and France was simply "granted" by the Big Three; China and France earned it by their contribution to the common struggle against the Axis powers. Neither

Roosevelt nor Churchill would otherwise have deemed it worthwhile to make the effort to include the two countries.

As early as July 1941, Roosevelt had proposed to Churchill to take the opportunity of the Atlantic meeting to issue a declaration laying down certain broad principles that should guide their policies along the same road. Both he and Churchill had in mind a special role to be played by the "English democracies" in whatever form of peacekeeping establishment after the war. The Atlantic Charter, which can be considered the prelude to the United Nations Organization, showed clearly this spirit. Starting with the Washington Declaration of the United Nations in 1942 all the way through to the 1944 Dumbarton Oaks Conversations and the resulting draft of the would-be UN Charter, almost all the preparatory discussions regarding the United Nations took place among the Big Three, as did subsequent controversies, negotiations, accommodations, and agreements. As victory over Nazi Germany came into sight, the situation became a scramble for spheres of influence between the Soviet Union and the West, though Roosevelt was less willing to recognize this fact than were Churchill and Stalin. The discussions prior to the Yalta Conference and the agreements signed at Yalta in 1945 marked the division of spheres of influence between the Big Three. Finally, at the San Francisco Conference minor adjustments to the structure of the United Nations were made in view of the dissatisfaction expressed by the smaller countries.

One of the principles recognized and advocated by all the sponsors of the United Nations was its universality. When controversies over membership arose, however, they were based, to a great extent, on the struggle for influence in which each of the Big Three spoke for or against a particular country or group of countries.

If we trace the principle of universality to the very beginning of the international organization, we see that the idea came from President Roosevelt, who put it into action with the help of US Secretary of State Cordell Hull and Churchill. All along, the position of the United States, especially of the Congress, carried no less weight than that of the other big powers. The influences that shaped the United Nations can be graphically described as a multi-level pyramid, with President Roosevelt on the top, the US government and the Anglo-American alliance on the second level, the Big Three on the third, the Big Five on the fourth, the eleven members of the would-be Security Council on the fifth, and the fifty-one signatories of the San Francisco declaration at the bottom. A line of American leadership thus runs from the top to the bottom.

Cooperation among the Big Three from the Washington Declaration to the Dumbarton Oaks Conversations

Pearl Harbor changed the balance of the power in World War II, especially the position of the United States. Now that the United States was fully involved in the war, the arguments for long-term isolationism were greatly weakened, and Roosevelt could proceed to fulfill his ideal of American leadership in shaping the postwar world: hence the Washington Declaration of the United Nations. It was drafted by Secretary Hull, agreed upon by Roosevelt and Churchill in consultation with the Soviet ambassador to Washington, signed in Washington by these three and the Chinese ambassador and ratified the next day by the twenty-two other countries fighting with the Allies. The layers of the pyramid can be seen distinctly through this process. From that point forward, President Roosevelt and the State Department began to formulate principles and structural procedures for a postwar international organization.

Naturally, everybody had in the back of his mind the failure of the League of Nations. For Roosevelt, the lessons from that organization were that there had been too great a diffusion of responsibility for decision-making, too many nations to be satisfied, and no police force to keep peace when necessary. Based on these concerns, he gradually developed a plan for an organization that was to be structured on three levels: a general assembly for all nations, the function of which would be to discuss all international questions and to advise the two smaller bodies; an advisory (or executive) council, comprising the big powers together with some six to eight other countries, which would make recommendations for settling disputes; and a small group made up of the United States, the United Kingdom, the Soviet Union, and China (France would come in afterwards), which would have the actual authority to deal with any threat to peace. The president believed that, in the end, "the real decisions should be made by the United States, Great Britain, Russia and China, who would be the powers for many years to come that would have to police the world."[1]

[1] Robert E. Sherwood, *Roosevelt and Hopkins: An Intimate History* (New York: Grosset

Roosevelt also advocated "diplomacy of principle," "moral disinterest instead of power politics" and expressed disapproval of the concept of "balance of power" and "spheres of influence." The Moscow Declaration of the Four Nations therefore sought to establish "a general international organization, based on the principle of the sovereign equality of all peace-loving states."[2]

In this context, the word "equality" had different implications for different countries. While the United States took upon itself the roles of spokesman and defender of rights for smaller nations, both Churchill and Stalin accepted the phrase with strong reservations. The United Kingdom had its own ideas, which stemmed from its own particular interests. After Pearl Harbor, one of Churchill's concerns was to "discourage bias towards the Pacific."[3] Understandably, he put emphasis on Europe and doubted the feasibility of concentrating power in a single executive group of great powers. He was in favor of creating regional bodies and advocated separate councils for Europe, Asia (or the Pacific), and the Americas. The United States would be involved in all three, and it went without saying that the United Kingdom would play the leading role among European countries. Another major ideological difference between the United Kingdom and the United States was over the question of independence and self-determination for colonial countries.

The Soviet Union had a concept of the postwar world different from the one vaguely envisaged by American policymakers. Early in September 1941, the Soviet ambassador to London, having spoken resoundingly in support of the principle of "self-determination of nations" and "the right of every nation to its independence [and] its territorial integrity," added that the Soviet government supported the consistent application of the principles of the Atlantic Charter, "considering that the practical applica-

---

and Dunlap, 1950), 717, quoted in Herbert Feis, *Churchill, Roosevelt, Stalin: The War They Waged and the Peace They Sought* (Princeton: Princeton University Press, 1957), 121.

[2] "Declaration of Four Nations on General Security," appendix D to Ruth B. Russell, *A History of the United Nations Charter: The Role of the United States* (Washington, D.C.: Brookings Institution, 1958), 977.

[3] Winston Churchill, *The Second World War,* vol. 4, *The Hinge of Fate* (London: Cassell 1951), 705.

tion of these principles will necessarily adapt itself to the circumstances, need, and historic peculiarities of particular countries."[4] This seemingly harmless sentence was in fact a significant reservation, preparing the ground for further Soviet acquisition of territories in the future. As the war went on, the Soviet Union gained increasing influence in proportion to its success and sacrifice in the resistance against fascist aggression. Its status as an equal partner with the other two big powers was finally established after the Battle of Stalingrad. As the Western nations counted more and more on the contribution of the Red Army on the battlefield, they became increasingly uneasy about the political intentions of the Soviet Union. The Anglo-American resistance to Stalin's candid territorial demands retreated step by step with the advance of the Red Army on the battlefield. By the time of the Tehran Conference, redefining boundaries according to the Soviet demands was a *fait accompli,* and the controversies remaining over this issue from previous meetings simply disappeared from the agenda. So, in this manner, the principle of "respect for territorial integrity" was taken care of.

For all their differences, Roosevelt, Churchill, and Stalin had one thing in common—the belief that postwar peace depended upon cooperation among their countries. Stalin was especially candid—even crude—in expressing this idea. He openly denied equal say to other countries. One of the arguments advanced by the Soviet Union in advocating absolute veto power for the Big Four/Five, was that the smaller powers ought not to be allowed to foment discord between the big powers by raising a dispute with one of them. The Soviet delegation was so adamant on this question that it could not be resolved at the Dumbarton Oaks Conversations and had to be deferred to Yalta. Although the United States and the United Kingdom opposed the Soviet position and finally succeeded in persuading Stalin to abandon it, one should remember that when Roosevelt first raised the idea of a postwar peacekeeping framework with Soviet Foreign Minister Vyacheslav Molotov in June 1941, he also suggested the necessity of controlling "smaller countries who had shown themselves disturbers of the peace in the past."[5] In essence, all three leaders advocated big power unanimity; they differed only in the degree to which the principle was to be carried out.

[4] Russell, *United Nations Charter,* 44.

[5] Feis, *Churchill, Roosevelt, Stalin,* 68.

Zi Zhongyun

The Balance of Power and Spheres of Influence: From Dumbarton Oaks to Yalta

The Yalta Conference established the framework for a postwar world based on spheres of influence. The agreements reached there also reflected the recognition by the Big Three of one another's relative strength. While these agreements temporarily settled the controversies, they sowed the seeds for endless disputes immediately after the war. Three major issues regarding the United Nations were unresolved at the conclusion of the Dumbarton Oaks Conversations: (1) the scope of veto power, (2) the initial members of the United Nations, and (3) territorial trusteeship. The discussion of these issues at Yalta reflected the different positions and interests of the three big powers. The first two issues pitted the Soviet Union against the two Western powers, while the third mainly affected the United Kingdom.

The crux of the disagreement over the veto lay in whether any one of the permanent members should retain its veto power when a party to a specific dispute. The Soviet Union insisted that it should, which meant absolute veto power for the permanent members. Stalin reasoned that nothing should be allowed to bring one of the Great Powers in conflict with the others; such a conflict, he argued, would undermine the cause of universal security. Stalin emphasized the vital importance of preserving unanimity without exception among the big powers from the start of any dispute. The Soviets were adamant on this issue in the beginning but finally agreed to a compromise offered by Roosevelt.

Stalin also initially demanded that all sixteen republics of the Soviet Union should be members of the United Nations with one vote each. He retreated to three additional seats and finally to two: Ukraine and Byelorussia. One can see clearly that Stalin's position on these issues stemmed from one concern: to protect the Soviet Union as much as possible against isolation in the future organization. Stalin was keenly aware of the minority position of the Soviet Union vis-à-vis the great majority of nations, which were under the influence of either the United States or the United Kingdom. His distrust of Western intentions ran deep.

The United States, on the contrary, enjoyed a sure and comfortable majority on its side. In addition to the nine Latin American countries that followed it into the war and subsequently signed the Washington Declaration, the United States proposed inclusion of eight other countries that had not fought the Axis. Six of them were again Latin American countries. The United Kingdom also sided with the United States, as did the British dominions, with whom most differences could be ironed out before being put to vote. In addition, the vote of China could be relied on in most cases. From this vantage point, Roosevelt could lecture both Churchill and Stalin that "the leadership of the great powers is to be based not alone upon size, strength and resources, but upon those enduring qualifications of moral leadership which can raise the whole level of international relations the world over."[6] On the other hand, he felt strongly the practical need for Soviet military cooperation in Europe and the Pacific, as well as in the postwar world. For these and other reasons, he showed more willingness than Churchill to accommodate Stalin.

Negotiations over trusteeship were carried out mainly between the United States and the United Kingdom. Partly because of the philosophical tradition of self-determination, which stemmed from the United States' history of independence, and partly because of his own awareness of the trend of the times, Roosevelt had always included in his blueprint for a postwar world organization an arrangement for self-government and independence for dependent territories. Either out of idealism or out of practical consideration of US interests—or both—he supported the aspirations of colonial peoples. This position clashed with that of the United Kingdom in general and of Churchill in particular.

The first test was over India. Understandably, American popular opinion was sympathetic to Gandhi and Nehru. Roosevelt first mentioned the subject to Churchill after Pearl Harbor, during the prime minister's first wartime visit to Washington. Churchill's reaction, however, was so strong that the President never dared mention it to him again. Roosevelt was rather discouraged by Churchill's famous remark in November 1942 that he had not "become the King's First Minister in order to preside over the liquidation of the British Empire."[7] Thus, the US government was caught in a dilemma: On the one hand, it did not want to be considered by the Indian and other colonial peoples as supporting British imperialism; on the other, it did not want to offend its most important ally.

[6] Ibid., 551.

[7] Russell, *United Nations Charter,* 82.

For a time, therefore, the position of the United States regarding territorial independence was ambiguous. While announcing the end of the age of imperialism and supporting the right of peoples to their freedom, the United States assured the British government that it would not do anything to undermine British authority over its empire. Against this background, the State Department put forward a compromise formula of trusteeship as a transitional step toward independence. With the approval of President Roosevelt, a draft "Declaration by the United Nations on National Independence" was produced. But the idea of national "independence" was unacceptable to the British, whose position was to maintain the empire. After much negotiation, the final text prepared for the Dumbarton Oaks Conversations by the State Department accommodated British demands by omitting all reference to national independence. This is evidenced by the chapter title: "Draft Declaration Regarding Administration of Dependent Territories." In addition, because of objections raised by the US military establishment, which sought to keep Japanese-occupied territories in American hands alone, the United States did not include the question of trusteeship in its proposals to the Dumbarton Oaks Conversations.

Resolution of the issue of trusteeship was postponed until the Yalta Conference. When the subject was brought up, however, Churchill objected so violently that Secretary of State Edward R. Stettinius, Jr. hurried to explain that this was meant for dependent areas that would be taken out of enemy control, not for the British empire. Churchill seized upon this explanation to ask for an explicit statement that trusteeship would not apply to dominions of the British empire.

Roosevelt kept silence the entire time, fearing that the United Nations project as a whole would be disrupted by a dispute over this single issue. The final document stated merely that the five permanent members of the Security Council would consult each other on the question of providing machinery in the Charter for trusteeships. On this issue, Churchill prevailed. Additionally, the US goal of ensuring that the islands taken from Japan be put under their sole trusteeship prevailed over considerations for the future of other dependent territories. The issue of trusteeship, therefore, was resolved by a compromise among the big powers. Both the wording of the final document and the American position were a far cry from the proclaimed noble idea of supporting the right to freedom for all peoples.

The Role of China and France: The Lesser Big Powers

China and France were by no means equal partners with the Big Three; in fact, their status as big powers was decided by the other three. At the suggestion of the United States, China was one of the four initial signatories of the Washington declaration and from that point forward had been counted among the Big Four. The United States wanted to include China for the obvious reason of encouraging China—at the time the only major independent state in Asia—to continue fighting the Japanese. From a long-term point of view, the US government by that time had already conceived its postwar strategic framework in eastern Asia, in which a strong and friendly China would be of vital importance to American interests, both to check Japanese ambition and to counterbalance the Soviet Union. Moreover, in the face of a rising tide of nationalism in Asia, both Roosevelt and the State Department wanted to avoid the impression that the Western powers intended to dominate the world.

Both Churchill and Stalin opposed granting China big power status; they thought her a secondary power and preferred to place priority on Europe. For Churchill, the "extraordinary significance" of China in American minds was "strangely out of proportion" to its true importance. He told Roosevelt that he could not be expected to accept the standard of values which accorded China a fighting power almost equal to that of the British empire.[8] Moreover, as he told British Foreign Minister Anthony Eden, privately, he feared that China would be a "faggot vote" on the side of the United States in any attempt to liquidate the British overseas empire.[9] It was with much reluctance that he finally acquiesced to the idea of China as the fourth power. The Soviet Union was even more adamant in its objections to including China among the major powers. In addition to the reasons advanced by the British, the Soviet Union had its own particular position because of its treaty of neutrality with Japan. At the Moscow Conference of 1943, Secretary Hull went so far as to hint that Anglo-American aid to the Soviet Union might be diminished in favor of China if China was excluded. This caused Molotov to relax his opposition.[10]

[8] Churchill, *Second World War,* 119.

[9] Ibid., 504.

[10] Russell, *United Nations Charter,* 134 n.

However, the signing of the Moscow declaration by the Big Four did not end the Soviet objection. The Soviet Union kept away from the 1943 Cairo Conference in order to avoid sitting with China, and when Stalin was shown the Cairo declaration before its announcement his reaction was one of "no comment." At the Tehran Conference, having declared formally the Soviet pledge to enter into the war with Japan after the defeat of Germany, Stalin tried again to oppose China's role as a global power by proposing regional committees similar to those put forward earlier by Churchill and rejected by the United States. Moreover, the steering committee at the Dumbarton Oaks Conversations consisted of only the United States, the Soviet Union, and the United Kingdom, while China came in for the last few sessions only to give approval to the tripartite agreement that had already been reached through long negotiations during almost two months of discussion. Finally, China was excluded completely from the Yalta Conference, where important deferred issues concerning the United Nations were finalized, not to mention the notorious secret agreements on the Far East by which China's interests and sovereign rights were bargained away by the Big Three behind her back.

France came into the picture later than China, and the disagreement surrounding its recognition as a major power was even more complex. The status of France—and attitudes toward General de Gaulle in particular— was a major point of controversy between the United Kingdom, on the one hand, and the United States and the Soviet Union, on the other. Churchill concisely stated his strategic interest in France to a group of senior American officials in May 1943. "It was important," he said, "to recreate a strong France; for the prospect of having no strong country on the map between England and Russia was not attractive."[11] Churchill also held an opinion different from that of Roosevelt and Stalin concerning General de Gaulle as a person. Despite personal antagonisms, Churchill recognized in de Gaulle the spirit of France and admired him as a symbol of the unconquerable French.[12] Therefore, the United Kingdom tried all along to connect France in one way or another with the prospective world organization. On the other side, both the United States and the Soviet Union strongly opposed the participation of de Gaulle's Free France until late in

[11] Churchill, *Second World War,* 717.

[12] Ibid., 611.

the process. Besides uncertainties as to de Gaulle's ability to rally the French, there was a well-known personal antagonism between Roosevelt and de Gaulle.

From the very beginning, Free France was excluded from the long list of nations invited to sign the Washington Declaration. A British suggestion to change the end of the document to enable the adherence of movements such as Free France was declined by Secretary Hull. By June 1942, however, after seeing that large segments of the French population were rallying to de Gaulle, the United States decided to deal with the French National Committee "as a symbol of French resistance in general against the Axis Powers," but only in matters related to the war. The Americans carefully avoided political recognition of de Gaulle's movement as the French provisional government. To bypass the delicate issue, the United States devised a formula by which the French would adhere to the "principles" of the declaration rather than to the declaration itself. De Gaulle, however, was not interested in anything short of full membership in the United Nations, so he declined the offer. Not until 23 October 1944, after the liberation of France and the unmistakable evidence of widespread support among the French people for de Gaulle, did the United States formally announce its decision to recognize the administration established in Paris under his leadership.

The Soviet Union had all along taken a scornful attitude toward France's actions during the war. Like Roosevelt, Stalin had little regard for de Gaulle and his movement. For pragmatic reasons, the Soviet Union issued a statement in August 1943 that formally announced a decision "to recognize the French Committee of National Liberation as representative of the state interests of the French Republic and leader of all French patriots struggling against Hitlerite tyranny."[13] Stalin revealed his true opinion of the French at the Tehran Conference, where he actually denied the existence of French resistance at all and regarded the Vichy government as the "real" France. Therefore, according to Stalin, France ought to be punished instead of being allowed to share in the benefits of peace.[14] However, like the United States, by the end of the Dumbarton Oaks Conversations the Soviet Union had changed its attitude toward France's status as a major power.

[13] Feis, *Churchill, Roosevelt, Stalin,* 315.

[14] Ibid., 316.

France became a member of the United Nations on 1 January 1945 after the conclusion of the Franco-Soviet Pact. Churchill was right in identifying de Gaulle with the French struggle for freedom from Nazi occupation. The change in attitude of both the United States and the Soviet Union towards General de Gaulle was based on the recognition of his support among the French people.

The San Francisco Conference and the Role of Smaller Countries

Until the San Francisco Conference, the smaller countries had had no say in the preparations for the world organization. By mid-1944, the consultations among the big powers on this matter, though not made public, began to cause concern among the smaller countries. On 9 June 1944, the Netherlands, Belgium, Luxembourg, and Norway addressed a memorandum to the Big Three expressing the desire of a large number of occupied countries to contribute to the settlement of German issues and to the formulation of political safeguards for their own future security. This was the first formal expression of misgivings among the smaller powers. At the same time, some Latin American governments also expressed their own concerns, in particular about the position of the inter-American system vis-à-vis the prospective world organization. San Francisco provided an opportunity for the smaller nations to air their dissatisfaction. The point in the Yalta formula that raised the strongest and most widespread objection at the San Francisco Conference was the veto power of the five permanent powers of the Security Council; however rationalized, the impression that the world organization would be dominated by the big powers could not be removed. Following a prolonged debate over the issue, a vote was forced through by the major powers.

Moreover, the discussion over membership constituted a typical reflection of the big powers' spheres-of-influence mentality. The main concern of the United States was to preserve its strong ties with the Latin American states. Therefore, when the Latin American countries expressed a strong desire to readmit Argentina to the American family of nations and to invite it to the San Francisco Conference, President Harry Truman agreed. The United Kingdom, supported by the United States, stood up for the members of the British commonwealth. Lest the Soviet Union renew its demand for the admission of all its republics, the United States and the

United Kingdom decided upon a distinction between the status of the British dominions and that of the Soviet republics and put the latter on the same footing as the fifty states of the United States of America. At the San Francisco Conference, the Soviets also sought to have the Lublin government of Poland admitted to the United Nations. While the United States and the Latin American countries put the seating of Argentina on the same ground as that of Byelorussia and Ukraine, Molotov argued that the seating of Argentina should be discussed together with that of Poland, implying a possible bargain between the two proposals. Finally, Argentina was admitted and the question of Poland was not even put on the agenda.

The question of the presidency of the conference also reflected the rising estrangement between the Soviet Union and the United States. The United States, with the support of the United Kingdom and China, took it for granted that as the host country, it should chair the conference. Molotov, however, insisted on a system of four rotating chairmen. The conference immediately reached an impasse over this issue. Finally, having failed to get a separate vote on his motion in the steering committee, Molotov accepted the compromise formula put forward by Anthony Eden whereby the chairmanship of the public meetings of the conference would be rotated among the four governments and Secretary Stettinius would be recognized as chairman of the steering and executive committees.

By the time of the San Francisco Conference, the world was already quite different from what it had been when the United Nations was conceived in 1941. World War II was followed by the Cold War, and the United Nations became a forum for often acrimonious debates between the two blocs. It is true that the United States was able to assure itself of leadership for many years by maintaining a sure majority in the General Assembly, but the ideal of big power cooperation gave way to rivalry between the two superpowers. Ironically, the veto system, which was designed to ensure big power unanimity on crucial issues, became an instrument for the Soviet Union to assert its rights from an isolated position. Over the years, with the addition of a large number of emerging nations, the idea of a big power assurance of peace further clashed with the principle of equal rights for all nations.

To what extent were the original expectations of the founders of the United Nations valid? How should the reality of differences in influence—and hence responsibility—between large and small nations in world affairs be reconciled with the ideal and principle of equality among all nations? Should there be a new group of "big powers" to reflect the new reality? How long can the present structure and procedural system based upon the original big power concept be maintained in a changed world? And what impact will the conflicting trends of globalization and reassertion of nationalism have on the functioning of the United Nations? These are the difficult questions confronting all members of the international organization today.

Collective Economic Sanctions: Nonforcible Responses to Threats to Peace

Lori Fisler Damrosch

The participants in the Dumbarton Oaks Conversations had to deal with the virtually universal perception that the League of Nations experience with economic sanctions had been an unmitigated disaster, or (to take just a few of the epithets from the literature on sanctions), a "great debacle,"[1] a "seminal failure, the generator of a whole series of other failures,"[2] even "the very midsummer of madness."[3] Few of their contemporaries any longer shared Woodrow Wilson's view of economic sanctions. In a passage that has become one of the quotable quotes on sanctions, Wilson had said, "A nation that is boycotted is a nation that is in sight of surrender. Apply this economic, peaceful, silent, deadly remedy and there will be no need for force. It is a terrible remedy. It does not cost a life outside the nation boycotted, but it brings a pressure upon the nation which, in my judgment, no modern nation could resist."[4] That view might have seemed

[1] David Baldwin, *Economic Statecraft* (Princeton: Princeton University Press, 1985), 154. The term "great debacle" is Baldwin's characterization of the bulk of academic and popular opinion; his own assessment is more balanced.

[2] Martin Wight, *Power Politics,* ed. Hedley Bull and Carsten Holbraad (New York: Holmes and Meier, 1978), 208, cited in Baldwin, *Economic Statecraft,* 154 n.

[3] Robin Renwick, *Economic Sanctions* (Cambridge, Mass.: Harvard University Center for International Affairs, 1981), 18, quoted in Gary Clyde Hufbauer, Jeffrey J. Schott, and Kimberly Ann Elliott, *Economic Sanctions Reconsidered,* 2 vols. (Washington, D.C.: Institute for International Economics, 1990), 2:39.

[4] Saul K. Padover, ed., *Wilson's Ideals* (Washington, D.C.: American Council on Public Affairs, 1942), 108, quoted in Hufbauer, Schott, and Elliott, *Economic Sanctions,* 9, and in

visionary in 1919, but by 1944 the league's unhappy experience had rendered it apparently illusory.

Of course the league's weak and brief sanctions against Italy did not prevent World War II. Nonetheless, scholarship in the present generation has given us the perspective to evaluate sanctions not just against some absolute measure of success or failure,[5] but also in relation to the range of policy options that could realistically have been applied under the same conditions.[6] Of the other strategies available to the league at the time of decision in 1935–36, neither the option of doing nothing nor the option of immediate military confrontation offered clearly superior alternatives. The problem was not necessarily with the concept of sanctions as opposed to inaction or immediate military force, but rather with the weakness of the sanctions implemented (especially the omission of oil from the list of embargoed goods) and the failure to signal that sanctions represented a first step in a continuum of coercive measures that could include military action if Italy persisted in violation of its obligations under the league covenant.

A further element of historical context will help us understand the thinking of the participants in the Dumbarton Oaks Conversations. While it is true that league sanctions were ineffectual in stopping the outbreak of World War II, it is at least equally true that economic measures (including trade embargoes and the blocking of financial assets) were critical to the Allies' strategies for winning the war once it became inevitable. Thus one of the building blocks of the plan for a postwar organization of collective

---

Barry Carter, *International Economic Sanctions: Improving the Haphazard U.S. Legal Regime* (Cambridge: Cambridge University Press, 1988), 9.

[5] One important reference work, which attempts to establish quantitative measurements for evaluating the effectiveness of sanctions, ranks the league's sanctions against Italy at the very bottom of a scale from 1 ("outright failure") to 16 ("significant success"). Hufbauer, Schott, and Elliott, *Economic Sanctions,* case 35-1. While such measurements are useful for various purposes, they shortchange the norm-reinforcing functions of sanctions and other normative dimensions. For a valuable critique, see Baldwin, *Economic Statecraft.*

[6] I refer here to the work of David Baldwin, who has offered a cogent reexamination of the league's sanctions against Italy under the heading "'Classic Cases' Reconsidered." Baldwin, *Economic Statecraft,* 154–65.

security was a system for rendering effective the application of collective economic pressure, in order to avoid war if avoidance were possible—but if war could not be avoided, then in order to wage it successfully.

The Treatment of Economic Sanctions at Dumbarton Oaks

On the subject of sanctions, the Dumbarton Oaks Conversations prefigured what became Chapter VII of the UN Charter and in particular Article 41 on measures not involving the use of force that could be undertaken in response to threats to the peace, breaches of the peace, and acts of aggression. (Article 41, of course, complements the other features of Chapter VII aimed at facilitating strong military measures.) The salient innovations included four important improvements over the league system.

First, the Dumbarton Oaks Proposals expanded the scope of situations capable of triggering the application of sanctions to include "threats to the peace" as well as "breaches of the peace" and "acts of aggression." Article 16 of the league covenant, in contrast, came into play only if a league member should "resort to war in disregard of its covenants." The league approach was clearly unsatisfactory, since only under extraordinarily fortuitous circumstances could mere nonforcible measures implemented after the fact bring about reversal of an act of war. In contrast, under the Dumbarton Oaks Proposals the new organization would be able to deal with threats to the peace on an anticipatory basis, with a greater expectation of forestalling the commission of actual breaches or acts of aggression. The Dumbarton Oaks approach makes it possible, for example, to contemplate using sanctions to thwart an incipient nuclear capability in advance, rather than waiting until after a state has not only completed its weapons project but actually started a war. Thus collective sanctions could now be invoked not only against a nation that has already invaded another, such as Iraq in 1990, but also against a country such as North Korea, whose nuclear activities pose a threat to peace wholly apart from any overt acts of warfare.

Second, the Dumbarton Oaks Proposals centralized decision making about economic sanctions in the newly constituted Security Council, including the authority to decide on specific compulsory measures. The league system was supposedly mandatory, by virtue of Article 16's provision that all league members "hereby undertake immediately to subject [the breaching state] to the severance of all trade or financial relations." However, in reality the league could not and did not order its members to fulfill these sweeping undertakings. It was left largely to each member's initiative and inclination to determine whether to adopt any measures at all.

At Dumbarton Oaks, the Soviet delegation proposed a catalogue of measures eventually incorporated in Article 41 of the Charter, which provides that the Security Council's measures may include "complete or partial interruption of economic relations and of rail, sea, air, postal, telegraphic, radio, and other means of communication, and the severance of diplomatic relations." The United States and the United Kingdom agreed to this proposal, overcoming their concern that such a listing might be viewed as a limitation on the council's powers. The final text is phrased permissively, and thus commentators agree that Article 41 "does not exclude the possibility of resort to other measures not enumerated . . . so long as they fall within the category of 'measures not involving the use of armed force'."[7]

Our current generation of problems has supplied examples of sanctions not explicitly identified in Article 41's catalogue but implicitly authorized by that article. Measures such as blocking of assets (invoked in the cases of Iraq, Yugoslavia, and Haiti either by the Security Council directly or by individual states acting in support of the council's policies) surely fall within the scope of Article 41. Practice now also supports the conclusion that the Security Council can set up a commission to adjudicate claims against a state, as it did with Iraq,[8] as well as the power to create a structure for allocating Iraqi assets and future oil revenues in support of UN-approved activities.[9] Another recent innovation in nonforcible measures is the creation of a war crimes tribunal, which the Security Council has done for the former Yugoslavia.[10]

[7] Leland M. Goodrich, Edvard Hambro, and Anne Patricia Simons, *Charter of the United Nations: Commentary and Documents,* 3d ed. (New York: Columbia University Press, 1969), 311–14, citing Ruth B. Russell, *A History of the United Nations Charter, 1940–1945* (Washington, D.C.: Brookings Institution, 1958), 466, 676.

[8] See Resolutions 674 (29 October 1990), paras. 8–9; 678 (3 April 1991), paras. 16–19; 692 (20 May 1991); 705 (15 August 1991).

[9] See Resolutions 706 (15 August 1991); 712 (19 September 1991); and 778 (2 October 1992).

[10] Resolution 827 (25 May 1993).

Third, the Dumbarton Oaks Proposals marked an advance over the league system by imposing an obligation—enforceable by coercive means if necessary—to implement the decisions of the Security Council. This introduction of a secondary level of coercion leads to the possibility not only of secondary boycotts of those who break sanctions[11] but also of using military force to enforce the sanctions themselves. This was done for the first time in 1966 with the authorization of the forcible interdiction of an oil tanker believed to be carrying contraband destined for Southern Rhodesia.[12] More recently, the Security Council explicitly authorized forcible interdiction measures with respect to Iraq, the former Yugoslavia, and Haiti.[13] Such measures not only improve compliance with the economic sanctions, but also signal to the target that economic sanctions are not a stopping point but rather a midpoint along a continuum of coercion that can include military force as well.

Finally, the Dumbarton Oaks Proposals also included the precursor of what is now Article 50 of the Charter, enabling states "confronted with special economic problems" arising from the carrying out of Security Council decisions to have "the right to consult the Security Council with regard to a solution of those problems."[14] The San Francisco Conference accepted this principle with the modification of the language to make clear that this right belongs to states other than those against which preventive or enforcement measures are being taken. The target, in other words, has no right to assistance in the solution of its economic problems.[15] The San Francisco modification did not, however, foresee today's generation of problems, in which unwanted effects on the civilian population in the target

[11] Secondary coercion has been discussed with respect to the Dominican Republic's failure to enforce the petroleum embargo against Haiti. See, for example, "Lean on the Dominican Republic," *New York Times,* 24 May 1994 editorial.

[12] Security Council Resolution 221 (9 April 1966).

[13] Resolutions 665 (25 August 1990) (Iraq); 787 (16 November 1992) and 820 (17 April 1993) (Serbia-Montenegro); and 875 (16 October 1993) (Haiti).

[14] "Dumbarton Oaks Proposals, Oct. 7, 1944," *Department of State Bulletin* 11, no. 276 (1944), 368, at Chap. VIII, sec. B, para. 11.

[15] Goodrich, Hambro, and Simons, *UN Charter,* citing *UN Conference on International Organization: Documents,* XVII: 207.

state constitute an ever-growing obstacle to both the effectiveness and the legitimacy of economic sanctions.[16]

There we have, in essence, the Dumbarton Oaks Proposals, calling upon members to respond to threats to peace with measures not involving the use of force. The proposals were accepted at the San Francisco Conference essentially unchanged and practically without debate.[17] They lay virtually dormant for forty-five years. With the conclusion of the South African elections, though, we can happily celebrate the second success of the two UN-imposed economic sanctions instituted during the Cold War, both involving apartheid.

Cases since 1990

A new era in the use of economic sanctions for collective security began on 6 August 1990, when the Security Council invigorated Chapter VII of the UN Charter in response to Iraq's invasion of Kuwait—a classic act of aggression. The Iraq sanctions remain in place today with a much more complex set of objectives: to ensure fulfillment of all cease-fire terms including disarmament and demilitarization, and also, at least implicitly, to induce Iraq to desist from repressing its Kurdish and Shiite minorities. In the brief but dense body of experience since 1990, we have seen a dramatic widening of the types of situations that have been treated as constituting "threats to the peace," situations that go well beyond the expectations of 1944.

In the years since August 1990, the Security Council has adopted compulsory economic sanctions in what has become an impressive array of programs. All of the former Yugoslavia was placed under a general and complete arms embargo in September of 1991.[18] In addition, stringent sanctions were targeted specifically at Serbia-Montenegro starting in May 1992 and have been strengthened and enforced in several subsequent reso-

[16] For discussion, see Damrosch, "The Civilian Impact of Economic Sanctions," in Lori F. Damrosch, ed., *Enforcing Restraint: Collective Intervention in Internal Conflicts* (New York: Council on Foreign Relations Press, 1993), 274–315.

[17] Goodrich, Hambro, and Simons, *UN Charter,* 311–14.

[18] Security Council Resolution 713 (25 September 1991).

lutions.[19] In the spring of 1993 the council sanctioned the Bosnian Serbs by prohibiting imports to, exports from, and transshipments through Serbian-controlled areas of Bosnia-Herzegovina. Certain controls also apply to transactions involving the UN-Protected Areas of Croatia.[20] The council has also strengthened the sanctions it had imposed on Libya in March 1992, in order to induce Libya to desist from support for international terrorism.[21]

Arms embargoes are currently in effect with respect to several areas of civil strife, notably Somalia since January 1992,[22] Liberia since November 1992,[23] and Angola since September 1993.[24] The Angolan embargo was targeted at UNITA for its failure to comply with obligations under previous resolutions. The supply of petroleum and petroleum products to UNITA is also prohibited. Following this pattern, the United States called for an arms embargo in response to the conflict in Rwanda.[25] These arms embargoes, targeted at civil wars and ethnic conflicts, are interesting examples of uses by the Security Council of its Charter-authorized power to deal not only with transboundary war in the traditional sense, but also with broader perceptions of threats to the peace.[26]

Perhaps most intriguing from the perspective of expanding conceptions of the Security Council's powers is the application of UN sanctions to Haiti. These had as their objective the restoration of the elected president, Jean-Bertrand Aristide, who had been overthrown in a military coup in September 1991. Security Council Resolution 841 of 16 June 1993 transformed what had been a regional, recommendatory sanctions program of the Organization of American States into a universal, mandatory

[19] For discussion, see Damrosch, *Enforcing Restraint,* 292, 297, 305.

[20] See Security Council Resolution 820 (17 April 1993).

[21] Resolutions 748 (31 March 1992) and 883 (11 November 1993).

[22] Security Council Resolution 733 (23 January 1992).

[23] Security Council Resolution 788 (19 November 1992).

[24] Security Council Resolution 864 (15 September 1993).

[25] See "UN Chief Seeks an African Peace Force for Rwanda," *New York Times,* 3 May 1994, quoting US ambassador Madeleine Albright on request for arms embargo.

[26] See Lori Fisler Damrosch, "Changing Conceptions of Intervention in International Law," in Laura Reed and Carl Kaysen, eds., *Emerging Norms of Justified Intervention* (Cambridge, Mass.: American Academy of Arts and Sciences, 1993).

one. In its 16 June 1993 decision, the council imposed an embargo on trade with Haiti in arms and petroleum or petroleum products, subject to certain humanitarian exceptions. The embargo was briefly suspended when it appeared that the *de facto* Haitian authorities were prepared to comply with their obligations to restore democratic governance. It was then reimposed in October 1993 when the illusion of compliance had disappeared.[27] Additional sanctions affecting trade and air transport were added in May 1994.[28]

The Haitian situation marked a new step in the Security Council's willingness to treat a domestic political crisis as a threat to international peace and security, and went farther than ever before in applying UN sanctions in support of domestic governance. Notably, China overcame its long-standing reluctance to support the use of Chapter VII in internal conflicts, and the several Haitian resolutions were adopted unanimously.[29]

Current Issues

The participants in the Dumbarton Oaks Conversations foresaw some of the issues decisionmakers are grappling with in the 1990s. As already noted, they envisaged that sanctions might cause unwanted harm to third parties, and they planned for a consultative process that might alleviate those difficulties. Solutions have not been easy to find. In the years since sanctions have taken off, there have been many dozens of petitions under Article 50 concerning billions of dollars of adverse third-country impacts, but little meaningful relief. However, enforcement procedures against Iraq were modified to substitute land-based inspections at the port of Aqaba in

[27] See Resolutions 861 (27 August 1993) and 873 (13 October 1993).

[28] See "UN Council Votes Tougher Embargo on Haitian Trade," *New York Times,* 7 May 1994, and "Haitian Generals Remain Defiant as a Strict Embargo Takes Effect," *New York Times,* 23 May 1994.

[29] Following the vote on Resolution 841, the Security Council president read aloud an agreed statement that "the adoption of this resolution is warranted by the unique and exceptional situation in Haiti and should not be regarded as constituting a precedent." See S/PV.3238 (16 June 1993), 9.

lieu of sea-based inspections, which Jordan claimed had been hurting its economy.[30]

It was understood, both at Dumbarton Oaks and at San Francisco, that it was open to the Security Council to use economic measures either in advance of forcible options or alongside them, or if necessary to proceed directly to force. Although the phrasing adopted at San Francisco differs slightly from the Dumbarton Oaks language,[31] commentators are in accord that the council need not wait for proof of inadequacy of nonforcible measures: "As was unanimously agreed at the San Francisco Conference, 'in the case of flagrant aggression imperiling the existence of a member of the Organization, enforcement measures should be taken without delay, and to the full extent required by the circumstances.' "[32]

The conversations at Dumbarton Oaks give us very little guidance, however, on what are turning out to be some of the most vexing problems of the current generation of sanctions. First is the humanitarian aspect or civilian impact problem, which I have dealt with in more detail elsewhere.[33] Sanctions need to be targeted to the maximum extent against actual wrongdoers and should be fashioned to avoid at least the most serious types of harm to vulnerable populations. The Dumbarton Oaks draft that became Article 41 is flexible enough to permit this kind of differentiated targeting. The question is how to achieve it. We are seeing a number of experiments, such as specific measures being directed at members of the *de facto* Haitian government. Special attention is also being given to the problem of effective provision of humanitarian relief.

Equally important is the problem of legitimacy. I refer not only to formal legal challenges, such as those brought in the International Court of Justice by Libya challenging the legality of coercive measures directed against

[30] "U.S. Accepts Jordan Plea on Iraq Trade," *New York Times,* 26 April 1994.

[31] As adopted at San Francisco, Article 42 contemplates that the Security Council can invoke forcible action when nonforcible measures "would be inadequate or have proved to be inadequate." The corresponding Dumbarton Oaks language was "Should the Security Council consider [nonforcible measures] to be inadequate."

[32] Goodrich, Hambro, and Simons, *UN Charter,* citing *UN Conference on International Organization: Documents,* XII: 507.

[33] Damrosch, "Civilian Impact."

it[34] and by Bosnia-Herzegovina challenging the validity of the Yugoslav arms embargo as an infringement of Bosnia's inherent right of self-defense under Article 51 of the Charter.[35] Under the heading of legitimacy, I also refer to the contention that UN members should be free to disregard a Security Council decision on the basis of their assessment of the situation, regardless of whether it has been able to prevail upon the council to endorse its own view. This line of argument was pressed with great vigor to urge the United States to disregard the Yugoslav arms embargo as applied to Bosnia on the basis of a controversial claim that Article 51 gives precedence to collective self-defense over council-ordered measures of collective security.

The sanctions effort concerning the former Yugoslavia shares with the league experience the dubious distinction of being widely perceived as not only an abysmal failure but even a counterproductive strategy. However, no matter how compelling the Bosnian case may be, the United States should not undermine the council's measures, except by persuading the majority of the council to lift embargo. Those who would encourage disregard for the council's compulsory measures will only erode the already fragile support for centralized international institutions, which are only now beginning to take on law enforcement functions. The long-term interests of the United States lie in strengthening, not undercutting, the enforcement capabilities of those institutions.

[34] In early 1992 Libya tried but failed to persuade the International Court of Justice to restrain members of the Security Council from moving forward with a sanctions program against it. See *Questions of Interpretation and Application of the 1971 Montreal Convention Arising from the Aerial Incident at Lockerbie (Libya v. U.K. and U.S.)* (Request for Provisional Measures, Order of 14 April 1992), 1992 I.C.J. 3, 114.

[35] The International Court of Justice has entered two preliminary orders on Bosnia's claim, relying in both instances only on the Genocide Convention and declining to take up broader questions under the UN Charter.

Sovereignty and International Intervention in the Internal Affairs of States: Peacekeeping Operations

Indar Jit Rikhye

Since the civil war in the Balkans in 1946, the UN Security Council has intervened in several internal conflicts on the basis of the UN Charter, declaring the crisis a threat to international peace and security. During the Cold War period, for example, the United Nations intervened in a succession of conflicts, notably in the Congo (Zaire) from 1960 to 1964, in Cyprus from 1964 until the present, in Lebanon in 1958, and in South Lebanon from 1978 until this day.

The two points that I wish to make with regard to intervention in internal conflicts are that the Security Council has a history of such interventions and that, because of the end of the Cold War and greater demands for action, efforts by the Security Council have increased considerably. The council has always tried to build consensus not only between the permanent members, who hold veto power, but also between other council members, whose votes are essential to obtain approval for action. The United States, taking the lead in most such situations, has had to work hard on members such as China and India, with their own human rights concerns, to persuade them to accept interventions.

The council has, however, cautiously avoided taking sides in the internal politics of states. In the Congo, for example, after the questionable removal of Prime Minister Patrice Lumumba by President Joseph Kasavubu in 1960 and the 1965 counter-coup by the army chief of staff, Joseph Desire Mobutu (Mobutu Sese Seko), it was the UN General Assembly's selection of the credentials of the president's delegation that determined the legitimacy of the head of the Congo's government. Once the political crisis had been resolved with the help of the United Nations and the US ambassador to the Congo, the United Nations conducted all its subsequent operations with the consent of the legitimized Congolese officials.

It is important to emphasize that the UN operations to end secession of parts of the Congo—of Katanga, in particular—were conducted with the full consent and support of the central government. As a general principle, when a constitutional or a recognizable authority acceptable under international law exists in an area of its operations, the United Nations obtains that government's consent and cooperation in the conduct of UN operations. Problems arise where authority is absent or fragmented; this was the case in Somalia, where the existing regime could be considered solely as *ad hoc* or *de facto,* but not a constitutional authority. Such situations are further exacerbated by the refusal of one or more of the *de facto* authorities to cooperate with the United Nations.

With the sole exception of the controversial UN action in Korea, the Cold War prevented enforcement actions provided for under Chapter VII of the Charter. The failure of the permanent members of the Security Council to arrive at a consensus led to the evolution of peacekeeping under Chapter VI of the Charter, facilitating the use of military forces in a peaceful role. This type of intervention required consent of the disputing parties. UN peacekeepers could use minimal force in self-defense only when all peaceful means had failed. The emerging rules of engagement worked satisfactorily in most instances.

It was in the Congo that the United Nations first met military defiance. The factionalized and ill-led Congolese army could hurt, but not seriously obstruct, UN operations; the European mercenary-led Katanga gendarmerie, on the other hand, presented a serious challenge to the United Nations Operation in the Congo (ONUC). The Katanga forces had virtually declared war on ONUC, which resulted in the operation becoming ineffective and having to take unacceptable casualties. The Security Council, in spite of the reluctance of some of the Western powers, authorized ONUC to use force for the removal of mercenaries, but only in self-defense in the last resort. This enabled ONUC to complete its mission. Nonetheless, the resolution remains controversial, some arguing that the use of force could have been authorized only under Chapter VII of the Charter.

It was the end of the Cold War that made use of Chapter VII feasible. Thus we have witnessed a number of enforcement operations authorized under Chapter VII, because, in the absence of due authority, consent of the parties is not always available. Moreover, factional leaders sometimes oppose UN intervention because—like General Mohamed Aideed of Somalia—they do not see it in their best interests.

Demands for UN intervention have increased enormously in recent years. Most regional efforts require UN support. The availability of television in millions of homes in many parts of the world has created immediate demands to help ease suffering. As a result, humanitarian relief and security have become major factors in international diplomacy. Since the end of the Cold War many crises have occurred in areas where few states have any legitimate interests. Neighboring states will often become involved in one way or another, but how should the global community respond to such disasters?

I believe the answer is clear. The human race has the responsibility to assist in every possible way to alleviate human suffering. Just as most advantaged people try to help those less advantaged, in international relations many fortunate and powerful states have similarly felt the obligation to help states that are less fortunate and that face disasters. The extent and the effectiveness of such aid will depend on prevailing conditions.

In the United States and elsewhere there is an increasing awareness that international intervention should be initiated with caution. An intervention using force requires even greater caution. While the US intervention in Somalia was laudable, it should be the exception rather than the rule, unless the United States or, for that matter, any other nation has direct interests at stake. Unilateral action is not the best choice; multilateral action is more likely to succeed. However, considering the costs involved and the low level of acceptability and enthusiasm for forceful intervention by the international community and by parties to these disputes, it is best to resort to such intervention only in exceptional situations.

The situation in Rwanda is a case in point. The United Nations intervened late, and as the situation worsened its peacekeeping troops became targets. This made the withdrawal of the UN troops inevitable. When its intervention is unwelcome, the United Nations has no choice other than to withdraw. Such a situation clearly signals that it is time for the guests to leave. A subsequent return to the area should only be considered when the circumstances have altered favorably for the United Nations.

Security for humanitarian assistance missions and nation-building tasks demands certain preconditions. An administrative structure and law and order remain essential. Without a governmental structure, only the use of force is needed to restore order. Where there is no governmental structure who is to exercise that authority? Who is the legitimate authority to invite the use of force to restore law and order? This is not the role desired by states without direct interests; even when they have such interests, they do not wish to be involved in fighting. It is for these reasons that UN enforcement operations authorized under Chapter VII of the Charter have so many reluctant warriors. The United Nations has attempted to overcome this problem by conducting peacekeeping along traditional lines, that is, under Chapter VI of the Charter, where the situation demands enforcement action.

I would suggest that the United Nations requires two types of troops: one for traditional peacekeeping under Chapter VI of the Charter and another for peace enforcement to deal with failed states and major disaster assistance. Furthermore, the United Nations does not require standing forces but rather a stand-by force. A large-scale enforcement operation as was conducted in the Persian Gulf should remain outside the organization's direct responsibility.

How should the United Nations organize these forces? The General Assembly has already completed a study on stand-by forces.[1] This should be followed by seeking volunteers for enforcement actions, a process likely to prove difficult. The United Nations should also continue with its efforts to develop training and greater state and regional participation. Finally, the UN Secretariat is already drawing up some essential guidelines for peacekeeping including rules of engagement, and operational procedures.[2] How-

[1] *Report by the Working Group on a Multinational United Nations Stand-by Forces High Readiness Brigade,* A/51/75–S1996/166 (5 March 1996). For updates, see the secretary-general's reports on stand-by arrangements for peacekeeping. UN docs. S/1996/1067 (24 December 1996) and S/1997/1009 (24 December 1997).

[2] United Nations Peacekeeping Operations, Lessons Learned Unit, *Multidisciplinary Peacekeeping: Lessons from Recent Experience,* 1996.

ever, the need to define command and control of peacekeeping forces deserves immediate and greater attention.

I am encouraged by the Clinton administration's policy on reforming multilateral peace operations.[3] The president's directive on this matter endorses many current UN practices that are acceptable to those countries contributing troops. The US administration defines what it considers threats to international peace and security, and will act provided that UN involvement advances US interests and that there is an international community of interest for dealing with specific problems on a multilateral basis. The United States would intervene when there is a threat to, or breach of, international peace and security, defined as one or a combination of the following: (1) international aggression; (2) urgent humanitarian disaster coupled with violence; or (3) sudden interruption of established democracy or gross violations of human rights coupled with violence or threats of violence.

There seems to be a general lack of understanding of command arrangements for peacekeeping operations, however. UN practice is as follows: All national contingents are under the command of their own commanders, following their own nation's military law and operational practices. The commander of the UN force is responsible for operational command, logistics support in the field, and general discipline. These command arrangements are governed by operational directives in accordance with the Security Council's resolutions and are conducted under the supervision of the council. Contributing countries and the United Nations have agreed to a number of different arrangements. The key to a successful UN command is no different from a national or an alliance command. It requires careful planning, consolidation, and coordination.

[3] Presidential Decision Directive no. 25 (3 May 1994), summarized in *International Legal Materials* 33 (May 1994), 795–812.

UN Peacekeeping during the Cold War: Middle East and Third World Perspectives

Walid Khalidi

In his final book, Richard Nixon recounts the last meeting he had with Mao Zedong in Beijing in February 1976. Mao, six months from death, had suffered a massive stroke which had rendered him virtually speechless. During the conversation, Nixon had said, "We must continue to cooperate in seeking peace, not only between our two countries but among the nations of the world." Mao snatched the notebook from his translator and wrote for her to translate, "Is peace your only goal?" Nixon had not expected the question, and after pausing briefly, replied, "We should seek peace with justice." Commenting on this incident some twenty years later, Nixon wrote, "My reply was adequate within the context of the cold war. Today, that is too limited a goal for the United States."[1]

The phrase "peace in our time" has had unsavory associations since September 1938, but the goal of peace, more than peace with justice, was the cornerstone of the Charter of the United Nations even before the Cold War. It is true that the principles of justice, international law, self-determination, and the sovereign equality of nations are all enumerated in Article 1 of the Charter. It is also true that the Charter describes, in Chapters IX and X, unprecedented collective concern for the "stability and well-being" of peoples, their standards of living, and their economic, social, physical, and cultural problems, as well as their human rights.

Nevertheless, the emphasis of the Charter, no less than the composition and the distribution of functions and powers among the main bodies of the United Nations, is on maintaining international peace and security.

[1] Richard Nixon, *Beyond Peace* (New York: Random House, 1994), 4.

This peace orientation was in part a response to the constitutional provisions in the Covenant of the League of Nations that had virtually "legalized" war in certain circumstances. It was also a reflection of the fact that the core members of the United Nations constituted a military coalition that had recently emerged victorious from the most horrendous war in human history.

Structurally, the United Nations was, at least in theory, better fitted for its task than the league had been. Through no fault of the league, the United States—the emerging global colossus—had not become a member, and the Soviet Union—the other emerging colossus—was a member only in the league's declining years from 1934 to 1939. Japan had resigned in 1932, Italy and Germany in 1939. The only two major powers that had remained members of the league throughout its existence were France and the United Kingdom. Thus, the gap in the distribution of power between those outside and those inside the league was so vast as to render questionable the insiders' ability effectively to influence events in Europe, much less in the rest of the world.

If the map of world realities facing the United Nations was composed of many overlays, the base map carried the imprint of two systems: the confederal system and the veto system of the permanent Security Council members, its logical extension under the circumstances. Both elements had been present in the league (the veto in a variant form) and had been its doing and its undoing.

In the United Nations, the price for preventing the recurrence of the league's predicament was the Security Council veto. Without the Security Council veto, there would have been no United Nations; with the Security Council veto, UN control over peace and international security was in the last analysis a *quinquevirate,* or, more accurately, a perennial consulate of two.

The veto system seemed to assume that major threats to international peace and security would emanate not from the permanent members, but rather from outside their circle. In the latter case, the permanent members would coordinate collective action in good faith against a disturber of world peace. It is difficult to believe that the imagination of the United Nations' founders was exhausted by this scenario, and one is driven to conclude that the peacekeeping edifice of the United Nations was built from the outset on a colossal but necessary pretense designed to enable the organization to see the light of day and give it a fighting chance.

To most of us, it is self-evident that an international organization such as the United Nations should aim at peace and be confederal in composition. However, it is humbling to reflect that these seeming verities were the culmination of a long European gestation that stretched back for centuries and engaged the minds of such luminaries as Cruce, Sully, Saint-Pierre, Bellers, Rousseau, Kant, Bentham, and Mill.

The reality of the Cold War promptly caught up with an organization still in its infancy. Indeed, the wartime camaraderie of the erstwhile allies did not last long. In February 1945 at Yalta, Winston Churchill was toasting Joseph Stalin—"The fire of war has burnt up the misunderstandings of the past"—and leading the British delegation in giving "three cheers for Marshal Stalin." Within a year, he was delivering his Iron Curtain speech at Fulton, Missouri. The Cold War struck all the more harshly because its principal protagonists were the two principal pillars of the new world order epitomized by the United Nations. These protagonists were not engaged in the traditional aristocratic diplomacy that had characterized relations between Britain and France (the two upholders of the League of Nations) in the interwar period, or Britain and Russia (the two upholders of the post-Napoleonic European *status quo*) in the nineteenth century. The United States and the Soviet Union were now locked into a confrontation that increasingly assumed a theological absoluteness constrained only by nuclear fears. Their arena was the entire globe, at which both looked almost exclusively through the prism of this confrontation. However, if nuclear fears set limits to direct conflict between them, they nonetheless proffered considerable leeway for competition and confrontation by proxy in Africa and Asia—a competition reminiscent of the nineteenth-century scramble for these regions that had also deflected conflict between the great European powers of that time.

Meanwhile, decolonization had been given a gigantic push by World War II, and it hit the nascent United Nations with no less force than the Cold War. As the repercussions of both phenomena interacted with one another, a whole new range of challenges and crises was spawned. Decolonization was one of the most extraordinary processes in human history. Overseas empires doggedly, laboriously, and ruthlessly built over several centuries were given up within a period of two decades by the imperial nations of Europe—Great Britain, France, the Netherlands, Belgium, Spain, and Portugal. It is sometimes forgotten that of all the sub-Saharan African countries currently members of the United Nations, only Liberia and South Africa were independent at the end of World War II, while none of the Arab countries of North Africa were independent except, technically, Egypt. Similarly, in Asia, apart from China and Japan, only a handful of countries between the Mediterranean and the Pacific were independent: Turkey, Yemen, Saudi Arabia, Iran, Afghanistan, Siam, and—again technically—Iraq.

It is not only that the independence of so many of the Third World countries inevitably revolutionized the composition of the United Nations; more important were the new challenges and responsibilities thrust on the organization as a result of the process of decolonization itself and the challenges resulting from its interaction with the Cold War. The process of decolonization was a messy one. In most cases the colonial powers had done little to prepare their former colonies for independence. Colonial frontiers were the result of deals between competing powers, arbitrarily ignoring geographic, economic, national, or ethnic factors, and constituted in themselves an ever-present potential for explosion. Although the rank and file of colonial armies were "native," the officers mostly were not, and the troops were recruited primarily from minority groups considered more dependent and therefore more loyal. The nationalist political elite tended to be long on ideology and fervor but short on administrative expertise. When the strong central authority of the imperial power was withdrawn, the centrifugal and conflicting forces created by the colonial system were released.

Concurrently, the vacuum created by the withdrawal of the imperial power encouraged the irredentist or imperialistic urges of regional neighbors, even as it beckoned to both Moscow and Washington. It is with the consequences of all this that the United Nations has found itself engrossed to this day. The attitude of the newly independent countries towards the United Nations was ambivalent, particularly at first. Memories of its predecessor were still strong. To the Afro-Asian countries, the League of Nations had been the club of the victorious imperial powers. The six Afro-Asian countries that had been among the league's thirty-two founding members were India (as one of five British empire representatives), China, Japan, Liberia, and Siam. Even towards the end, in 1938, only eleven of fifty-eight league members were Afro-Asian.

The league had been responsible for the mandate system, a system imposed by force and within which there was no avenue for redress. The league's watchdog over the mandatory powers—its Permanent Mandates Commission—had eleven members, drawn mostly from the imperial powers themselves and their allies. Only one of the eleven was Afro-Asian—Japan. At the San Francisco Conference in 1945, only twelve out of fifty delegations were Afro-Asian.

As the Afro-Asian component of UN membership leapt in number, some of these early reservations dissipated. Nevertheless, the attitude of the Afro-Asians towards the United Nations remained ambivalent. On the one hand, there was the perception of the organization as a buffer against the powerful, a source of economic and technical assistance, a fire brigade in extreme exigencies, and a forum for articulating fears and grievances—indeed, for cocking the snook at the powerful themselves. On the other hand, there was the perception of the United Nations as the preserve of the industrial countries. Its specialized agencies were seen as weighted in favor of countries whose unannounced agenda was to maintain the economic, technological, military, and commercial asymmetry between themselves and the Third World and whose trumpeted international morality was vitiated by favoritism, selectivity, and double standards.

The Afro-Asian states' self-image of victimization (partly a carryover from pre-independence colonial days anchored in genuine or imagined grievances) fed on the growing gap in well-being, achievement, and development between the First and Third Worlds, a gap that was itself a function of the intrinsic qualitative gap in governance and economic management between them.

Consciously or unconsciously, this perception of victimization served as an alibi for the failure of a Third World leadership largely addicted to variants of one-party rule and economic statism, a failure that exposed independence on which so many hopes had been pinned as the sham it had become. Concurrently, this self-image was fueled by the dialectic of the Cold War, the attempt of one superpower at containment and of the other at leapfrogging over it. Afro-Asia and, to a lesser extent, Latin America were now viewed as a chessboard on which the superpowers, in their obsessive preoccupation with each other, aspired for exclusive advantage away from the more sensitive areas of nuclear confrontation.

All this found expression in the main bodies of the United Nations and its subsidiary and affiliated organs—in blocs and counter-blocs, and in strident and symbolic resolutions and counter-resolutions that remained fundamentally exercises in frustration. Given the configuration of power in the world, America's shoulders were draped with the mantle of post-independence neo-colonialism and indeed of pre-independence colonialism. This, in turn, elicited angry growls of protest and increasingly emphatic references to the confederal infrastructure of the United Nations and the primacy of national interest over perceived supranationalism. It led to the withholding of assessments and warnings of withdrawal. It is against the background of these realities that successive secretaries-general, dedicated international civil servants, and the thousands of peacekeeping observers, soldiers and civilians sent overseas have had to operate.

What can be learned from a survey of the United Nations' performance in maintaining international peace and security? If one looks at all UN peacekeeping missions, both past and current, one is struck by the following: There have been more peacekeeping missions in the six years since the end of the Cold War than in the previous forty years of the Cold War itself: thirteen missions during and twenty since. Of the thirteen missions during the Cold War (1948–88), the vast majority (ten) fall within the Middle East, in its wider definition to include the Indo-Pakistan frontier; the remaining three were the missions in West Irian (1962–63), the Congo (1960–64), and the Dominican Republic (1965–66). Of the ten missions in the Middle East, the majority (six) involve the Palestine problem and the Arab-Israeli conflict; the missions in Lebanon (1958), in Yemen (1963–64), on the Indo-Pakistan border (1949, 1965–66), and in Cyprus (1964–present) make up the remaining four.

In looking at the UN missions that took place during the Cold War, one is immediately struck by the circumscribed geographic area within which they were allowed to operate. Outside this area (with the few exceptions mentioned) the superpowers set the pace extramurally, so to speak. Where they did so, the United Nations neither had nor could have had a meaningful role. Thus the Soviet interventions in Hungary in 1956, in Cuba in 1962, Czechoslovakia in 1968, Angola and Ethiopia during the mid-1970s, and in Afghanistan in 1979. Thus the United States' actions in Vietnam, in Libya offshore and onshore in 1986, and in Central America in the 1980s (Grenada, Nicaragua, El Salvador, Panama, and the Dominican Republic).[2] It is no coincidence that when the United Nations did intervene in some of these areas, it was after the end of the Cold War.

Korea was *sui generis*. It was possible only because of the fortuitous—or perhaps not so fortuitous—Soviet absence in the Security Council and the ingenious Uniting for Peace resolution under the determined leadership of the United States. Ninety percent of the so-called UN forces were American and South Korean, with the real power coming from the United States. What the United Nations supplied was the legal and moral cloak around the US forces that made it easier for Moscow and Beijing to come to terms, especially given the threat of still greater use of American might.

The most remarkable UN operation outside the Middle East during this period and since is the Congo. Its distinctiveness lies in the extent to which the United Nations' success in snatching the Congo from the jaws of disintegration and the Cold War was due to the breathtaking resourcefulness and perseverance of Dag Hammarskjöld in the face of hostility from the Soviets. At the cost of his life, he demonstrated how the organization could be more than the sum of its parts.

Within the largely circumscribed area in which UN missions operated during the Cold War period, three of the conflicts addressed by these missions—the Palestine problem, Cyprus, and the Indo-Pakistan border—were as close to political intractables as you can get. It is not easy to select a yardstick for measuring the United Nations' success or failure in handling these intractables. For India and Pakistan, Kashmir epitomized the lingering trauma of partition in 1947. The Greek-Turkish divide in Cyprus was imbued with the entire weight of a history that went back five hundred years to when Constantinople became Istanbul. While the Palestine question as a modern political conflict was not anchored in ancient enmities, its evolution has awakened them.

In both the Indo-Pakistani and the Arab-Israeli cases, and to a lesser degree in the case of Cyprus, the intractability of the conflicts was rein-

[2] In some of these instances inter-state forces were present, and in the case of the Dominican Republic a UN observer force was installed.

forced by the alliances between the protagonists and the superpowers. The matter was further complicated by the varying attitudes of the superpowers to the UN peacekeeping role itself, the United States being generally supportive and the Soviet Union wavering between a desire to participate and open hostility. This hostility is exemplified in Moscow's *troika* proposal to replace the secretary-general in 1960 and the subsequent crisis over the Soviet Union's contributions. Yet another complication in the Middle East was Washington's determination until 1973 to keep the Soviets out of any peacekeeping mission there.

It is not surprising therefore that the role of the United Nations on the Indo-Pakistani frontier, in Cyprus, and in the Arab-Israeli conflict was limited. Some find disquieting the fact that the presence of peacekeeping forces neither prevents conflicts from reerupting nor facilitates their resolution. Some even believe that the presence of such forces contributes to the intractability of these conflicts, while at the same time excusing the protagonists from reaching a settlement and lulling the world into a false sense of security.

Thus, the detractors argue, the 1965 war broke out on the Indo-Pakistani border despite the Military Observer Group (UNMOGIP). The Turkish invasion of Cyprus in 1974 took place despite the Peace-keeping Force (UNFICYP). Border raids continued unabated in the Arab-Israeli conflict during the 1950s and 1960s despite the Truce Supervision Organization (UNTSO). The 1967 war broke out despite the Emergency Force (UNEF-I), and in 1982 Lebanon was invaded despite the Interim Force (UNIFIL).

What such criticism misses is that these forces were installed because no political solution to the conflicts could be reached. It also misses the fact that in concept, mandate, numbers, equipment, and mission these peacekeeping forces were never meant to stop invading armies or large-scale raids; nor could they have even if they had been designed to do so.

Although limited, the peacekeeping role of the UN has often been significant and sometimes crucial as a fig leaf, a face-saver, a moral buffer, a red line of sorts, an intermediary, an alibi, or a *deus ex machina*. The UN forces helped to prevent major war in Cyprus between 1960 and 1974 and again in years following. In India, they helped prevent it between 1949 and 1965 and again after 1965. In the Golan, the Disengagement Observer Force (UNDOF) has presided over a Scandinavian calm between Syria and Israel.

In at least three instances in the Middle East—in 1949, 1956, and 1973—the UN peacekeeping role was crucial. In 1949 the acting mediator in a *tour de force* of ingenuity and sheer hard work, brought about the Armistice Agreement. While the armistice left intact the core of the conflict, it put an end to large-scale hostilities until the outbreak of the 1956 Suez war.

In that war, the tripartite invaders Britain, France, and Israel had no option, given President Dwight Eisenhower's insistence on the restoration of the *status quo ante,* but to withdraw. The Suez venture had in a sense been Britain's imperial swan song, a nostalgic striving to preserve the Middle East as its special domain, not only against pan-Arabism but against the superpowers as well. France, reeling from Dien Bien Phu and increasingly beleaguered in the Maghrib, saw in Gamal Abdel Nasser the architect of its torment in Algeria. To David Ben-Gurion, the opportunity to destroy Egypt's new arsenal and demilitarize the Sinai in a military coalition with Britain and France was the mother of windfalls. It was, of course, the US stand and not the Soviet rocket-rattling that thwarted all these hopes.

Hence, UNEF-I, a *deus ex machina* enabling the invaders to withdraw with minimal ignominy. However, UNEF was installed in only one host country: Egypt; Israel refused the stationing of the peacekeeping force on its own soil. Finally, the October 1973 war had produced a situation between the superpowers even more potentially explosive than the 1956 war. In their counter-offensive, the Israelis had crossed the canal, and the Egyptian president, Anwar Sadat, had appealed to the United States to enforce a cease-fire. Sadat was also considering an appeal to both superpowers for joint action. Moscow made massive troop movements and demanded, as in 1956, joint military action with the United States. Washington declared a nuclear alert. Against this background, the cease-fire finally came into place and UNEF-II to supervise it. As in 1956, it was the UN peacekeeping force that was the *deus ex machina.*

UNEF-II became the model for UNDOF on the Syrian front. The Soviets did not get their joint military forces, but for the first time they did get military observers and Warsaw Pact (Polish) peacekeepers. UNEF-II manned the buffer zones between the Egyptian and Israeli disengagement lines from 1974 until the Camp David accord. UNDOF has been manning the buffer zone on the Syrian side since then. Of course, none of this would have been possible without the full commitment of US power and persuasiveness—the pity is that there was no room in Secretary of State

Henry Kissinger's conceptual scheme of things for the Palestinian core of the problem.

U Thant, the secretary-general at the time, has been faulted for his handling of the 1967 Middle East crisis that had been triggered by Nasser's request on 16–17 May for the immediate withdrawal of UNEF-I from Sinai and Sharm al-Sheikh (on the Gulf of Aqaba). While the secretary-general informed the advisory committee on UNEF of the legal necessity of complying with Egypt's request, he repeatedly warned Nasser of the likely consequences via the Egyptian UN ambassador and proceeded to Cairo himself on 22 May. It was while he was *en route* that Nasser publicly announced the closure of the Strait of Tiran. Nasser's actions provided Israel with its *casus belli,* despite the fact that Egypt was within its legal rights to demand such withdrawal and irrespective of whether Nasser was really bent on war.

Critics of U Thant have faulted him for not ordering UNEF-I to stay put and for not exercising his right under Article 99 to summon the Security Council to consider a situation threatening to international peace and security. The former criticism ignores the fact that UNEF was beginning to disintegrate; the contingents of India and Yugoslavia, allies of Egypt, automatically complied with their host's request. The latter criticism, while more valid, probably underestimates the likely immobility of the Security Council due to the superpowers' calculations. The deeper causes of the June war lay, of course, in the non-resolution of the Palestine problem. This had been exacerbated in the mid-sixties by the diversion of the Jordan River and by the rise of the Palestinian guerrilla movement, itself an index of a new Palestinian generation's despair at the international community's indifference to their plight.

The superpowers were otherwise engaged, their attention focused on the mounting tragedy of Vietnam. The interplay between Vietnam and the Middle East in the superpowers' calculations at this time remains to this day relatively unexplored. Symbolic of their passivity in the crucial days after Nasser's fateful miscalculation is the image of a secretary-general, with few carrots and even fewer sticks, on a lone pilgrimage to Cairo to ward off singlehandedly the coming hurricane.

The proliferation of UN peacekeeping missions since the end of the Cold War reflects the erosion of the old constraints; it also reflects a growing consensus on the relevance and utility of these missions. Talks have been underway on a UN inventory of peacekeepers and equipment for future operations and on guidelines for these operations. This is as it should be. The new era presents the world with a daunting array of new challenges: the deepening malaise of Third World countries, the implosion of some societies towards anarchy, the strife within and across borders resulting from the breakup of previously coherent entities, and the emergence of brutally willful regional powers. In response, a new generation of peacekeeping missions has been born, which has added to the earlier functions an unprecedented range of responsibilities in the political, civil, social, and humanitarian fields. A more forthright enforcement role for the peacekeepers is being articulated.

This again is as it should be if expansion of the circle of chaos is to be checked. The United Nations is the natural repository of an international ethos and the seat of its institutional memory. A special responsibility rests on the First World to sustain this orientation with innovative prudence. For the First World to lapse into solipsistic indifference or selectivity is to betray the very foundations of Western civilization.

Humanizing Global Institutions

Mahbub ul Haq

For too long, the principal focus of the Bretton Woods institutions and the UN system has been on the processes of economic growth, not on the enrichment of human lives. It was quietly assumed that high levels of economic growth would automatically translate into high levels of human development.

We know now that this may or may not happen. There is no intrinsic link between economic growth and human well-being. What is critical is which sections of society participate in the process of economic growth, who benefit from it, and what the character and distribution of this growth are. The quality of growth is just as important as its quantity.

The practical experience of nations demonstrates this reality. Oman enjoys three times the per capita income of Costa Rica but only one-third its literacy rate, a life expectancy lower by ten years, a more degraded environment, and few political freedoms. Sri Lanka and Guinea have the same gross national product (GNP) per capita according to the 1993 *World Bank Atlas:* $500. Nonetheless, contrast the quality of life in their societies: a life expectancy of seventy-one years in Sri Lanka but only forty-four years in Guinea; an adult literacy rate of eighty-nine percent in Sri Lanka and only twenty-seven percent in Guinea; an infant mortality rate of twenty-four per one thousand in Sri Lanka and as high as one hundred thirty-five in Guinea.[1] This is because it is not only the level of income that counts; it is how that income is spent by a society. Human beings make many choices—social, cultural, and political—that are independent of their wealth. Income is important, but it is far from being the sum total of people's lives. People

[1] *World Bank Atlas* (Washington, D.C.: International Bank for Reconstruction and Development, 1993).

are searching, therefore, for new models of human development that treat GNP growth as a means—not as an end—that enhance human life, replenish natural resources for future generations, and encourage individuals to participate in the events and processes that shape their lives.

The issue is not growth *per se,* but its character and distribution. Those who postulate a fundamental conflict between economic growth and human development do a disservice to poor nations. Economic growth is clearly not an option in addressing poverty; it is an imperative. But what type of growth? Who participates in it? Who benefits from it? These are the real issues. To benefit the masses, growth opportunities must be equitably distributed. They must also be sustainable from one generation to the next.

The concept of sustainable development is fairly simple. It is based on equal access to development opportunities for both present and future generations. The heart of this concept is equity within and between generations—but an equity of opportunity, not necessarily an equity of results. What people do with their opportunities is their own concern, but they should not be denied an equal opportunity to develop their human capabilities. Such equity requires many structural reforms: better distribution of productive assets, including land and credit; open access to market opportunities; a policy environment conducive to job-creation; and social safety nets for those who are bypassed by the markets.

The emerging concern with sustainable development takes this dialogue a step further. Development opportunities must be provided not only to present generations but to future generations as well. This does not mean protecting every form of natural capital or every resource or every species; if more efficient substitutes are available they must be used. What must be protected, however, is human life. We must never forget that mankind is the most endangered species on earth. Economic growth and environmental protection are only means: the real end is human welfare.

What must be sustained for the next generation is the capacity to enjoy the same level of well-being that our own generation possesses. The concept of sustainable development, therefore, focuses attention not only on the future but also on the present. There is something distinctly odd in worrying about yet unborn generations when the present generation is poor and wretched. There is also something immoral about sustaining present levels of poverty. Development patterns that perpetuate today's inequities are neither sustainable nor worth sustaining. Indeed, global sustainability without global justice is an elusive goal.

The policy implications of sustainable development are profound. A major restructuring of the world's income and consumption patterns—especially a fundamental change in the current lifestyles of rich nations—may be a necessary precondition for any viable strategy of sustainable development. Investment in people should be regarded as the most productive form of investment, and the allocations of global financial and development institutions should reflect this recognition. At present, approximately ten percent of World Bank allocations are earmarked for human priority concerns—i.e., basic education, primary healthcare, safe drinking water, adequate sanitation, essential family-planning services, and nutrition programs. The World Bank, to its credit, has been increasing the share of its total resources to such essential human priorities for some time now.

However, the present balance between physical and human infrastructure needs further correction. What is more, the World Bank needs to persuade its recipients to allocate more resources for basic, rather than higher, education, for rural health centers rather than only for urban hospitals, and for low-cost water supply and sewage schemes for rural areas. The need for such reorientation is even greater in regional development banks. For example, the African Development Bank currently allocates only four percent of its total resources to human priority concerns despite the fact that Africa has some of the lowest human development indicators in the world.

Another major factor in creating sustainable development is changing the policy conditionality of the Bretton Woods institutions. Both the World Bank and the International Monetary Fund have suffered a good deal of criticism for the conditionality of their structural adjustment programs. It is often suggested that the social and human costs of their adjustment programs have often been harsh and excessive. This argument requires dispassionate analysis.

The heart of an adjustment program generally is the better balancing of a nation's books—a gradual balancing of its budget and a reduction in its excessive borrowing. There can be no denying the need for such an adjustment program in most developing nations. What is important is whether a better budget balance is reached through the expansion of supply or only through demand management. In poor nations, there is little consumption to deflate.

Naturally, it is much better if a country is given enough time to expand its GNP and to grow into a new balance. What is even more important is what expenditures are cut in a budget—military expenditures and subsidies to the rich or financial support for social services and food subsidies to the poor. Governments in the developing countries often cut subsidies to the poorest and politically weakest groups in society and then blame their actions on the policy conditionality of the Bretton Woods institutions.

I have had a good deal of experience in these negotiations from both sides—for twelve years as a staff member of the World Bank and for eight years as the finance and planning minister in Pakistan. I do not believe that the World Bank staff chuckles in the middle of the night over the so-called harsh human conditionality of their loans. What really happens is that the developing country governments find it politically convenient to squeeze the poorer and weaker sections of society and pretend that doing so is part of external conditionality.

The Bretton Woods institutions must also accept their own part of the responsibility in this game of mirrors, however. They must pressure governments to cut military rather than social spending—something they have started doing only in the last few years. They must analyze subsidies to high- and low-income groups in a national budget and stand firm on slashing subsidies to the rich, elitist groups in a society before subsidies to the poor are touched. They must spend as much time discussing politically sensitive issues such as land reform and corruption as they do now on distorted prices in the economic system. These are not easy issues; some will be politically distasteful. However, unless the Bretton Woods institutions are willing to take some political heat on these issues, the cause of the poor—always weakly defended in their own systems—will go by default in implementing adjustment programs. Sub-Saharan Africa is a good example of this. From 1960 to 1992, the region increased its military spending from 0.7 percent of its total Gross Domestic Product to 3.5 percent—about five times—while many African countries cut their spending on education and health during the adjustment period of the 1980s.[2]

[2] United Nations Development Programme, *Human Development Report, 1993* (New York: Oxford University Press, 1993).

It is also time for the United Nations to act on the concerns that its annual *Human Development Reports* have introduced into the global development dialogue. Several steps are needed for this purpose. The UN secretary-general has already proposed an Agenda for Development that will serve as a unifying theme for all UN development efforts. The heart of this agenda should be the new models of human development.

My personal view is that it would be logical to establish a single integrated human development agency within the United Nations by merging all UN development funds—UNDP, UNICEF, UNFPA, IFAD, and WFP.[3] Such an agency would have command over as large a pool of resources as the International Development Association—about $5 billion a year. Moreover, these funds would be grants, not credits, so that there would be a substantial net transfer of resources to developing countries. Such an outright merger is not a very popular proposal with development agencies that have built up separate mandates, constituencies, and staffs. The second-best solution would be greater policy coordination between these agencies through a common policy board and a common field office under the unified umbrella of human development.

The UN system can provide technical assistance to developing countries to help them formulate their own long-term human development strategies. In the final analysis, however, the ownership of the new development strategies must belong to the developing nations themselves.

During the next fifty years, the role of the United Nations will need to be fundamentally different from its current one. Conflicts are now within nations rather than between them—as many as seventy-nine out of the eighty-two conflicts during the 1980s. More than ninety percent of conflict-related casualties are now civilian.[4] Many nations are now beginning to disintegrate from within—for example, Somalia, Bosnia, Angola, and Haiti. The 1994 *Human Development Report* presents a depressing forecast of about seventeen potential trouble spots around the globe that may be heading for violent internal conflicts.[5] In such a *milieu,* we need to engineer a "second

[3] These are, respectively, the Development Programme, the Children's Fund, the Population Fund, the International Fund for Agricultural Development, and the World Food Programme.

[4] United Nations Development Programme, *Human Development Report, 1994* (New York: Oxford University Press for the United Nations Development Programme, 1994).

[5] Ibid.

birth" of the United Nations—a far greater focus on human security rather than territorial security. Instead of a permanent police force, the United Nations must organize a permanent peace corps; it cannot continue to fight the battles of tomorrow with the weapons of yesterday.

This was clearly foreseen by the founders of the United Nations. In June 1945, when US secretary of state Edward Stettinius reported to President Truman on the establishment of the United Nations, he had the foresight to observe, "The battle of peace has to be fought on two fronts. The first is the security front where victory spells freedom from fear. The second is the economic and social front where victory means freedom from want. Only victory on both fronts can assure the world of an enduring peace. . . . No provisions that can be written into the Charter will enable the Security Council to make the world secure from war if men and women have no security in their homes and their jobs."[6]

The Cold War obliged the United Nations to preoccupy itself with the first front during its first fifty years. The organization does not have a brilliant record on dealing with the second front. The social summit in Copenhagen in 1995 provided a unique opportunity to construct the base of this second pillar of human security. The role of the United Nations must be strengthened in the development field in order to deal with the basic causes of internal conflicts.

It is also my firm conviction that an economic security council must be set up within the United Nations as the highest decision-making forum to deal with threats to global human security and to agree on necessary remedial actions. Such a council must deal with all issues confronting humanity—from food security to environmental security, from global poverty to jobless growth, from international migration to drug trafficking. While its total membership should be kept small and manageable, it should represent all world constituencies and carry no country veto. It should oversee the policy direction of all international and regional institutions, including the Bretton Woods institutions. It must be staffed by the ablest professional staff, formulating enlightened policy options on the economic

[6] US Department of State, *Charter of the United Nations: Report to the President on the Results of the San Francisco Conference by the Chairman of the United States Delegation, the Secretary of State* (26 June 1945), pub. 2349, conf. ser. 71 (Washington, D.C., 1945), 109.

and social dilemmas facing mankind. In fact, democratic global governance for the twenty-first century and the introduction of new models of sustainable development are inconceivable without such an economic security council.

The emerging emphasis on human development and sustainability of human life will lead to many significant changes in the policy dialogue and assistance strategies of global institutions; I have touched upon only a few of these implications. We still have a long way to go in humanizing global institutions.

Human Rights from Dumbarton Oaks

Louis Henkin

Those who planned the commemoration of the 1944 Dumbarton Oaks Conversations decided to devote one of very few sessions to human rights. That decision presumably reflects the view that concern for human rights is an important development in international life in the past half-century and that it had its roots at Dumbarton Oaks in 1944. The Dumbarton Oaks Proposals did indeed provide—almost incidentally—that the projected international organization should, among much else, promote respect for human rights. The international human rights movement, therefore, may plausibly be seen as a sturdy tree grown from one of the small acorns scattered at Dumbarton Oaks fifty years ago. However, the movement's development could hardly have been foreseen, even by the most hopeful or prescient of the participants in the conversations.

The "framers," I suggest, would have no reason to be surprised by the United Nations' action against aggression in the Gulf War in 1991; they would have reason to be very surprised by its actions in support of human rights in Somalia and Haiti, or by the 1994 debates as to whether the United States should deny most-favored-nation status to China because of its gross violations of human rights.

The anniversary of the 1944 conversations inspires celebration. It suggests also inventory, as well as anticipation—an agenda for the future. International human rights deserve all three.

Human Rights before Dumbarton Oaks

Before World War II, how a country treated its own inhabitants was no one else's business. In principle, indeed as a matter of principle, the condition of human rights in any country—even in Hitler's Germany—was not the concern of the international system, of international politics, or of international law.

Glimmers of change appeared early in World War II. After aggression in Europe but before the United States entered the war, President Franklin Roosevelt articulated his famous Four Freedoms. Shortly thereafter, Roosevelt and Winston Churchill alluded to freedom from fear and want in the Atlantic Charter. However, the Atlantic Charter expressed war aims and was commonly recognized as a weapon of psychological warfare. "Realists" did not take it seriously as policy for the postwar.

Human Rights at Dumbarton Oaks

Records of the Dumbarton Oaks Conversations contain no evidence that the principal participants, in thinking of the world order after the war and in planning for a new international organization, thought much about human rights. Somehow, someone introduced eight words among the secondary purposes of the organization-to-be: to "promote respect for human rights and fundamental freedoms."[1] This is the first use of "human rights" in a major document. Thus began what some might describe as the subversion (if not the end) of state sovereignty. Thus was born the idea that how a nation treated its own inhabitants was—in principle, as a matter of principle—everybody's business, the business of the international system, of international politics, and of international law. In those eight words, I suggest, lay a commitment to the idea of human rights, and to international responsibility to address gross violations of human rights anywhere. I do not think it far-fetched to trace to those eight words the entire human rights edifice built during the past half century.

Those beginnings at Dumbarton Oaks were small and promised little, but they led directly to the UN Charter, as well as to the Nuremberg Charter. In the UN Charter the eight words became several sentences, including Articles 55 and 56—a pledge by members to take action to promote "universal respect for, and observance of, human rights and funda-

[1] *The United Nations: Dumbarton Oaks Proposals for a General International Organization*, Department of State Publication 2297, Conference Series 66 (Washington, D.C.: Government Printing Office, 1945), Chap. IX, sec. A, para. 1.

mental freedoms for all without distinction as to race, sex, language or religion." The Nuremberg Charter established that there were crimes against humanity not based in any treaty and that those who perpetrate such crimes might even be hanged as a result. From Nuremberg there is also a direct line to the international tribunal that the Security Council established in 1993 to address war crimes in the former Yugoslavia.

The beginnings at Dumbarton Oaks were small in another sense. The commitment to human rights was small. If, we assume, President Roosevelt (and later President Harry Truman) and Winston Churchill were committed to human rights, we need hardly ask about Joseph Stalin (or even Chiang Kai-shek). Even if the United States and the United Kingdom, however, were committed to human rights at home, were they equally committed to international human rights, to giving the term international definition, to promoting such rights vigorously, as part of the new order, by any necessary means? It is far from clear that they were committed to participating in the international human rights movement, to establishing an international law of human rights applicable to all, including themselves, or to creating and submitting to effective international monitoring and enforcement.

Still, I suggest, one can trace a path from Dumbarton Oaks to international human rights at the end of the twentieth century: from human rights as psychological warfare to human rights as the idea of our times; from ringing rhetoric to an international bill of rights; from the universalization of that idea in the Universal Declaration of Human Rights to its internationalization in the International Bill of Rights.[2] One might trace a path from Dumbarton Oaks in 1944 to the new South Africa in 1994 and to collective responsibility and action (or inaction) in Somalia, Haiti, Bosnia, and Rwanda; from Dumbarton Oaks to the UN High Commissioner for Human Rights. I will highlight a few "markers" on these uneven paths.

From Dumbarton Oaks to the Universal Declaration

The Universal Declaration of Human Rights may be the second most important international instrument of the century, after the United Na-

[2] The International Bill of Rights is the appellation commonly used for the Universal Declaration and its two covenants taken together.

tions Charter. Its principal contribution, I believe, is that it universalized the idea of human rights, bringing "constitutionalism" into the constitutions of 185 states.

The Universal Declaration also transformed a phrase and an idea into an authoritative catalogue of rights. Neither the Dumbarton Oaks Proposals nor the UN Charter defined human rights. Behind the Universal Declaration were national bills of rights, but the declaration improved on them: to the United States Bill of Rights, for example, it added the fruits of two hundred years of Supreme Court interpretations. The Universal Declaration had behind it Franklin Roosevelt's Four Freedoms, but those seem almost quaint today, written when those who thought of human rights thought of freedoms of speech and religion, not of freedom from genocide, and murder, and abduction, and torture. Building on Roosevelt's legacy and his fourth Freedom—the freedom from want—the Universal Declaration added the rights of the welfare state as well as democracy.

From universalization, the Universal Declaration made its way into internationalization, to an international law of human rights through covenants and conventions, and to international institutions—from the Human Rights Commission envisaged by the Charter, to the Human Rights Committee under the Covenant on Civil and Political Rights and its counterparts under other covenants and conventions, to the recently established UN High Commissioner for Human Rights to regional courts and commissions in Europe and the Americas and an African Commission on Human and Peoples' Rights. One might trace a path from Dumbarton Oaks also to the end of Communism and the establishment of democracy as the prevailing ideology in the world today. One can trace a path even from "promoting" human rights at Dumbarton Oaks to enforcing them by collective humanitarian intervention (in Iraq, Somalia, and perhaps Haiti).

One can even see a path, errant but traceable, from Dumbarton Oaks to 1994's human rights triumph: the new South Africa. South Africa represents every major facet of the international human rights movement conceived at Dumbarton Oaks. South Africa is an instance of universal commitment to the principle of human rights; of law, not by treaty (since the Republic of South Africa was not party to any relevant treaty), but imposed by the conscience of the international system on a resisting state; of international responsibility for implementing human rights; of international monitoring and enforcement by sanctions that were not without effect.

The UN Organization and Human Rights

Perhaps in the spirit of celebration I have traced plausible human rights paths from Dumbarton Oaks to the international human rights condition today. I do not suggest that the roads from Dumbarton Oaks have not been bumpy. The United Nations organization proposed a half century ago did, however, help promote respect for human rights by committing states to the human rights idea and by sponsoring the Universal Declaration, the covenants, and numerous conventions.

Even in celebration, however, one cannot give the United Nations three cheers. It deserves applause for the excellent standards of the Universal Declaration—a noble monument both during and since the Cold War—but the United Nations is a political body and it has reflected the politics of enforcement and non-enforcement, the reluctance of states to monitor and be monitored. The implementation system promoted by the United Nations remains primitive. Especially during the Cold War, the political organs judged politically and applied double standards and selective targeting. The organization could not even respond to genocide in Cambodia and equatorial Africa. Moreover, for thirty years the Soviet Union led a willing coalition in opposition to the idea of a UN High Commissioner for Human Rights.

The Cold War is now over, but in the changed world order the United Nations is not yet clearly committed to implementing the human rights law it has created. In June 1993, China led a group of countries that sought to undermine this international commitment by challenging the universality of human rights in the name of "cultural diversity," and the commitment to implement human rights in the name of state "sovereignty." Efforts to prevent the establishment of the office of the UN High Commissioner for Human Rights did not succeed, but the mandate of the office was weakened, its resources reduced, and the commitment to effective monitoring rendered questionable.

For the United States too, the commitment it made at Dumbarton Oaks remains less than firm. Human rights are secure in the United States, but we are not wholly committed to international human rights. We committed ourselves to promoting respect for human rights, not only for others, and not only when it did not cost much to do so. We continue to resist ratifying covenants and conventions, and we load those that we do ratify with unnecessary reservations, understandings, and declarations. We are reluctant to lead and to bear the various costs of collective implementation. The Clinton administration's latest policy directive does not promise US leadership or support for UN actions against human rights violations any more than for peacekeeping.[3]

Refugees and Their Human Rights

The Dumbarton Oaks Conversations and the fifty years since they took place have failed to address one major human tragedy of our times: the plight of refugees. The international system had failed refugees before World War II; it did little for them afterwards. Even the excellent Universal Declaration has failed refugees. It recognizes the right to seek asylum and to enjoy it, but it does not recognize unambiguously a right to receive asylum so that it can be enjoyed. The noble effort resulting in the 1951 Convention relating to the Status of Refugees[4] gives no refugee any right to asylum. An incidental provision committing states to *non-refoulement*—not to send a refugee to a country of oppression—gives a refugee that much, but no right to be admitted for haven.[5] Furthermore, the US Supreme Court cut down that little bit by declaring that the obligation of *non-refoulement* applies only to refugees already in a state's territory and does not prohibit reaching outside its territory (as on the high seas) to return a refugee to oppression or death.[6]

The refugee remains the stepchild of the human rights movement. Many millions of refugees are victims of our "compassion fatigue." There is no sign that the international system can mobilize itself to address their tragedies; to develop programs for discouraging refugee-flow by monitor-

[3] Presidential Decision Directive no. 25 (3 May 1994), summarized in *International Legal Materials* 33 (May 1994), 795–812.

[4] 189 U.N.T.S. 137 (28 July 1951).

[5] Ibid., Article 33.

[6] *Sale v. Haitian Centers Council, Inc.*, 509 U.S. 155 (1993).

ing and improving human rights conditions; to provide foreign assistance to discourage an exodus of economic refugees; to develop a firm right of asylum for at least some refugees and some obligations to share the burdens of asylum; to help states see that they have a "national interest" in recognizing and respecting the human rights of refugees.

An Agenda for the Next Century

There is need for an agenda for human rights in the next half century. I do not suggest an effort to overcome the weaknesses that the Cold War engendered. The Universal Declaration is a masterful document, but it suffers the defects of its birth during the Cold War. It does not recognize a right to individual autonomy generally, its commitment to democracy is ambiguous (designed to be acceptable to "people's democracies" as well as to authentic constitutional democracies), and it recognizes economic welfare rights but not economic freedom. It is necessary to tighten the provisions in the Covenant on Civil and Political Rights providing for derogation in emergency. There is also a need to address human rights during civil war and in failed states.

I would not, however, tamper with the Universal Declaration or the covenants; I believe they can be tightened by enlightened interpretation. The principal item on the human rights agenda must be to make real the commitment to human rights and to realize these rights in fact. Prominent on the agenda must be the achievement of the promised equality of women, which is essential to human dignity (and to the right to development).

Once the system encouraged ratification of covenants regardless of reservations. We saw the virtue of promoting adherence even if it was hypocritical. Is it now time to reject reservations and to insist on *bone fide* compliance? Is it not time to achieve effective implementation, beginning with efforts to make the UN High Commissioner effective? Is it not time to remind all states that the condition of human rights everywhere is their business and that gross violations anywhere are detrimental to their national interest? It is necessary to achieve commitment on the part of the major powers—the United States, Japan, and the European powers—to act against gross violations.

Dumbarton Oaks can be proud of what began within its walls fifty years ago. Eight small words launched a remarkable, revolutionary program—the universalization of the idea of human rights and the excellent standards prescribed in the Universal Declaration bringing the promises of constitutionalism, the rule of law, democracy and rights into each of nearly two hundred constitutions. There is even some commitment to international responsibility, to some institutions, and some "machinery," to induce states to honor their commitments and respect and ensure human rights.

An English author described someone as having the harried look of a cook who knew that one cannot feed people once and for all. The problems of human rights and of refugees cannot be solved once and for all; the effort continues. It can be celebrated as having begun at Dumbarton Oaks half a century ago.

Individual Rights, Minority Rights, and Group Rights

Alain Pellet

As is well known, peoples' rights were absent from the Dumbarton Oaks Proposals; they were added only later, mainly at the insistence of the Soviet Union. Peoples' rights are mentioned twice in the United Nations Charter: in Article 1, paragraph 2 and Article 55, both of which refer to "the principle of equal rights and self-determination of peoples."

These same provisions deal with "human rights and fundamental freedoms," but as a distinct concept. One might have questioned, then, whether the drafters of the Charter considered peoples' rights as constituents of human rights. However, these doubts faded with the adoption in 1966 of the UN covenants on human rights; the covenants refer to the right of self-determination, which must therefore be considered at least as closely bound to human rights and, probably, as a collective human right in itself.

Although the inclusion of the right of self-determination in the covenants was decided as early as 1954, the relationship between self-determination and other rights has long been obscured by the exclusive use of the principle of self-determination as a tool to favor decolonization. While all the relevant instruments of the General Assembly (including Resolutions 1514 [XV] and 2625 [XXV]) and the covenants themselves paid lip service to the right of "*all* peoples" to self-determination, the use of that right was in effect limited to colonial and other assimilated peoples who were the victims of foreign occupation or domination. Moreover, the application of the right to self-determination to occupied or dominated peoples has remained narrowly circumscribed; it has in fact been applied only to the Palestinian people and the South African (and, for a short time, the Southern Rhodesian) black majority. It is significant that the United Nations never expanded this right to Afghanistan or Lebanon, for example, when there were good grounds to do so.

The reasons for this are obvious: When there were only a few colonial powers, many states in the international community feared that their own territorial integrity or national unity would be threatened by international recognition of the existence of different peoples among their own population. Moreover, a majority of states found it unacceptable to recognize that citizens could have rights against the state, which had long been recognized as the sole subject of international law. States were the only legal entities entitled to exercise rights and to incur legal obligations at the international level.

In order to sustain these prerogatives, the United Nations confined the exercise of the rights of peoples within very rigid limits. First, as noted above, it limited the exercise of the right to self-determination to colonial peoples strictly defined. Second, once decolonization was achieved, formerly colonial peoples were granted no additional rights at the international level (at least no more *real* rights). From the moment of decolonization, the rights of the people concerned were supposed to be exercised by the state. Third, the right to decolonization was, in fact, equated with the right to independence. Despite the fact that it had proclaimed that "the free association or integration with an independent State or the emergence into any other political status freely determined" by the people were means to achieve decolonization,[1] the United Nations in fact favored quasi-exclusively the establishment of sovereign and independent states. Finally, great precautions were taken to maintain the territorial integrity of states, peoples, and territories. Of course, this could be seen as contradicting the principle of a right to independence. This contradiction was resolved through the legal proposition that "the territory of a colony or other non-self governing territory has, under the Charter, a status separate and distinct from the territory of the State administering it."[2] Therefore, independence in the framework of the colonial borders does not undermine the territorial integrity of the administering power.

[1] *Declaration on Principles of International Law concerning Friendly Relations and Cooperation among States,* General Assembly Resolution 2625 (XXV) (24 October 1970).

[2] Ibid.

One would have thought, consequently, that the right of peoples to self-determination would have been fulfilled with the realization of political decolonization, which, with very rare exceptions, is an indisputable reality today. Such a view is erroneous. In the first place, this was certainly not the intent of the drafters of the Charter. Peoples' rights are in no way limited by the Charter to colonial peoples; indeed, no such link appears anywhere in the Charter, and it is clear from the *travaux préparatoires* that the drafters of the Charter did not intend so narrow an application. Many of the most influential states represented at the Dumbarton Oaks Conversations and San Francisco Conference were themselves colonial powers, and they would certainly not have accepted such a suicidal principle. It is only because of the changes in world politics and balance of power that the shift in the interpretation of the right to self-determination occurred. In fact, what "self-determination" meant was clearly "democracy," even though there was no agreement on the meaning of this term among the drafters. Second, it has been affirmed repeatedly that all peoples—not only colonial peoples—have a right to self-determination. Third, the changes in the world order—in particular political decolonization, the collapse of Communism in Eastern Europe, and the spread of political liberalism and pluralism—have favored a new reading of the Charter that is probably more in accordance with the original meaning of peoples' rights.

It is premature to try to describe in any detail the new legal situation, but trends can be seen even if they are not yet consolidated. The central idea is certainly that the right of all peoples to self-determination must not be and is not an empty formula. The problem is that the Charter nowhere defines what constitutes a "people," nor is there any universally accepted definition. In fact, as James Crawford has aptly said, "peoples rights embodies a category, not a definition. What constitutes a people may be different for the purposes of different rights."[3] Furthermore, principles of equal rights and self-determination do "not imply that the category 'peoples' rights' requires that the term 'peoples' should have the same meaning for the purposes of all rights accepted as falling within the category."[4] This seems

[3] James Crawford, "The Rights of Peoples—Some Conclusions," in James Crawford, ed., *The Rights of Peoples* (London: Oxford University Press, 1988), 170.

[4] Ibid., 166.

very sensible and entirely in keeping with the contemporary practice of the United Nations, even if the legal definition of 'peoples' is far from completely clear at this date.

The present trends are as follows: First—and this must be stressed again—*all* peoples have a right to self-determination whether they are colonized, under foreign domination, or a minority. Second, such a right does not imply a right to independence; it does so only for colonial or assimilated peoples. Other categories of peoples certainly do not have such a right, and it is significant that neither the United Nations nor any other international forum has proclaimed any right to independence in favor of minorities in the former Yugoslavia or the former Soviet Union. The 1992 Declaration on the Rights of Persons Belonging to Minorities does not hint in any manner at such a possibility, although it shyly envisages that minorities—and not only the persons belonging to minorities—can hold certain legal rights.[5] Third, it seems quite clear that minorities are considered increasingly as "peoples," as is shown by the term "indigenous peoples," a special category of minorities clearly established by the practice of the UN Human Rights Committee on the basis of Article 27 of the 1966 Covenant on Economic, Social, and Cultural Rights. Minorities and indigenous peoples also are being recognized as having specific rights that do not, however, amount to a right to sovereignty. Finally, apart from specific peoples that constitute minorities and indigenous peoples, the present practice of the United Nations suggests that all groups that show a real coherence and share a similar view of their own future and the same global values have special rights. The two most important of these rights are the right to self-identity (i.e., the right of all individuals who see themselves as part of the group to be recognized as such) and the right to democratic governance and participation.

This latter right remains in its infancy. However, efforts by the United Nations in recent years to send missions to monitor and control democratic electoral processes in various countries and the adoption by the General Assembly of a series of resolutions calling for "enhancing the effectiveness of the principle of periodic and genuine elections" clearly tend in this

[5] General Assembly Resolution 47/135 (18 December 1992).

direction.[6] The UN operations in Cambodia, for example, are also evidence of this same trend.

If a conclusion may be drawn from all this, it is the following: Far from having disappeared with colonization, the right of peoples to self-determination has gained a new vigor with the changes in the world order. It is now up to the United Nations and its member states to consolidate the trend toward democratic governance and participation and to make the principle as strong a tool for reinforcing democracy as it used to be for facilitating decolonization. This would be in keeping with the intent of the Charter's framers, who first met at Dumbarton Oaks fifty years ago.

[6] General Assembly Resolutions 44/146 (25 December 1989), 45/150 (18 December 1990), 46/137 (17 December 1991), and 47/138 (18 December 1992).

Universal Human Rights in a Multicultural World

Rein Müllerson

Do international human rights standards really reflect, if not exclusively then at least basically, only Western values, as some authors maintain,[1] and does cultural relativism, asserting that "evaluations are relative to the cultural background out of which they arise"[2] mean that these rights and freedoms, or at least elements of them, are alien to non-Western countries?

The "Statement on Human Rights" published in 1947 on behalf of the executive board of the American Anthropological Association[3] and submitted to the UN Commission on Human Rights, emphasized the Western cultural bias of the draft UN Declaration on Human Rights: "It will not be convincing to the Indonesian, the African, the Indian, the Chinese, if it lies on the same plane as like documents of an earlier period. The rights of man in the Twentieth Century cannot be circumscribed by the standards of any single culture or be dictated by the aspirations of any single people."[4]

Certainly, ideas of human rights emerged in Western countries; consequently, Western concepts made the largest contribution to the elaboration of the major human rights instruments after World War II. Of course, in support of the universal character of basic human rights, it is possible to

[1] See, for example, A. D. Renteln, *International Human Rights: Universalism versus Relativism* (London: Sage Publications, 1990).

[2] M. Herskovits, *Man and His Works* (New York: Alfred A. Knopf, 1950), 63.

[3] *American Anthropologist* 49 (1947), 539–43.

[4] Ibid., 543.

refer to the fact that by 1966 (the date of the adoption of the international covenants on human rights) not only the Soviet Union and other so-called socialist countries but also most Third World states had already been able to influence the content of these documents, which are now freely ratified or adhered to by considerably more than one hundred states, the majority of which are non-Western countries.[5] Does this almost universal and, what is even more significant, cross-cultural adherence to the most important international human rights instruments testify irrevocably in favor of the universality of international human rights standards?

Abdullahi Ahmed An-Na'im, who himself, no doubt, is genuinely concerned with human rights, especially in Muslim societies, and who does not by any means defend these societies' human rights records, writes of basic UN human rights instruments that "we should not assume from the fact that governmental delegates 'participate' in their formulation and adoption that there is necessarily sufficiently broad popular acceptance of these standards, and commitment to their implementation, in our respective countries."[6] In other words, those who signed and ratified universal human rights instruments on behalf of non-Western states either did not know what they were doing or were simply hypocrites. Of course, it may be that they were genuinely trying to help their peoples enjoy human rights and to change traditions and practices that were not conducive to these rights or that may in themselves have constituted human rights violations.

All three of these reasons may have informed the ratification of these instruments by some countries; I am sure that the Soviet Union or other so-called socialist states, for example, would not have changed their practices and laws simply because they were signatories to universal human rights treaties. Leaders of these countries behaved hypocritically and arrogantly in giving their consent to be bound by these instruments. However,

[5] For example, by the end of 1993 the International Covenant on Civil and Political Rights had 124 states party (74 of these had signed Optional Protocol no. 1, under which individuals have an access to the Human Rights Committee); the Covenant on Economic, Social and Cultural Rights had 120 states party; the Covenant on the Elimination of All Forms of Racial Discrimination had 137 states party. I thank Mr. A. Tikhonov of the UN Centre for Human Rights for this information.

[6] A. A. An-Na'im, ed., *Human Rights in Cross-Cultural Perspectives: A Quest for Consensus* (Philadelphia: University of Pennsylvania Press, 1992), 428.

this in itself does not mean that the reason for discrepancies between freely adhered-to obligations and actual practice lies in the cultural bias or any other deficiency of universal human rights instruments.

Even more important than formal consent is the fact that when one goes beyond rather general assertions that the cultural, religious, and historical traditions of a given country should be taken into account in assessing its human rights record, one can hardly say specifically to what extent generally accepted international human rights standards conflict with cultural or religious values of individual societies. In some cases, as we will try to show below, certain practices that are rooted in cultural or religious traditions and that contravene universal human rights standards are not accepted any more unanimously in the societies where such practices still take place.

Sometimes those who deny the very possibility of the existence of universal human rights in the multicultural world simply miss the point. I would agree, for example, with the foreign minister of Singapore, Wong Kan Seng, who in his statement at the World Conference on Human Rights in Vienna said that "universal recognition of the ideal of human rights can be harmful if universalism is used to deny or mask the reality of diversity."[7] Does recognizing the universality of human rights really mean that it is necessary to reject the obvious cultural diversity of the world? The foreign minister stated that "Singaporeans, and people in many other parts of the world do not agree, for instance, that pornography is an acceptable manifestation of free expression or that a homosexual relationship is just a matter of lifestyle choice."[8] However, here he is comparing the values of his own society, as understood by him, not with universal human rights standards but with values of some other societies. Neither the freedom to distribute pornography nor equality between homosexuals and heterosexuals in all domains are universal human rights norms. Indeed, many controversial issues—the death penalty, euthanasia, abortion, pornography, homosexuality, etc.—touch upon deeply rooted moral and religious sentiments and are treated differently in various societies. Notwithstanding the close relation of these issues to human rights, there are no universal standards

[7] "The Real World of Human Rights," statement by Foreign Minister Wong Kan Seng of Singapore at the World Conference on Human Rights, Vienna, 16 June 1993, 2.

[8] Ibid., 4.

guaranteeing or prohibiting such acts, though, of course, certain of these acts may, by implication, in themselves qualify as human rights violations. Here, if you like, cultural relativism has its point.

The Iranian representative to the United Nations office at Geneva, at the end of the UN Human Rights Committee's consideration in October 1992 of the report on civil and political rights in Iran, stressed the need to take into account the cultural criteria of any country in assessing its human rights record. At the same time, he confirmed that the International Covenant on Civil and Political Rights and the Universal Declaration on Human Rights were compatible with Islam.[9] (Though I would have preferred to hear that Islam is compatible with these instruments, I respect and understand this view.) The emphasis on cultural criteria simply missed the point, especially because the members of the Human Rights Committee did not question the cultural values of the Iranian people or of Islam.[10] Can one justify the persecution of Baha'is, the death penalty by stoning for adultery, mutilation as a punishment, and the *fatwa* against Salman Rushdie as cultural requirements that should be taken into account while speaking of human rights in that country? It is true that some fundamentalist religious concepts are in fact incompatible with international human rights instruments (to the extent that these instruments mandate equality between men and women or tolerance of other religions)? Even here, I would assert, we can hardly discern any imposition of specific Western values or approaches on culturally different societies.

Christian fundamentalism in this respect is not much different from its Islamic counterpart. Western European countries have a long history of discrimination against women, and in many European countries heretics were burned at the stake. The Spanish Inquisition was abolished only in 1834,[11] and in 1925 a school teacher was condemned by a local court in Tennessee for teaching Darwin's theory of the origin of man.[12] Regarding the punishment of crime, Western European countries *have* moved from such cruel forms of execution as hanging or guillotining to the complete abolition of the death penalty, but the main difference between the two

[9] UN Press Release HR/3215, 30 October 1992 (afternoon), 1.

[10] Ibid.

[11] *Longman Illustrated Encyclopedia of World History* (London: Ivy Leaf, 1991), 463.

[12] Ibid., 410.

religious fundamentalisms is that while the Christian one was powerful in the Middle Ages, the rise of Islamic fundamentalism is a contemporary phenomenon.

The receptiveness of different societies to international standards of human rights is conditioned less by the cultural peculiarities of a given society than by the level of that society's social, economic, and political development. How people are executed—whether hanged, stoned, or guillotined—or tortured depends to a great extent on a specific culture, but whether people are executed or tortured at all depends more on the level of societal development. However, if only a hundred years ago those who used hanging to punish criminals did not know much about those who used stoning, today the world has become too small and interdependent to expect that only missile technology or computer hardware and software can transgress state boundaries. Human rights have the same capacity for dissemination among different peoples.

Contemporary human rights standards are not immutable values inherent only in Western countries. Western countries themselves, and others as well, came to accept these values through a long process. In traditional societies, be they Eastern or Western, the individual could fulfill his or her human dignity only according to his or her position in the society. In these societies, the very notion of individual autonomy was absent, and traditional societies could have neither human rights nor even a concept of them.[13] It was the emergence of the modern state and the market economy that mandated liberal concepts of human rights.[14] The emergence of market economies made individuals autonomous not only vis-à-vis each other but also vis-à-vis society; this meant that a degree of individual autonomy vis-à-vis the state was also needed. However, the state, absent guarantees of individual autonomy in the form of human rights, has a propensity to encroach upon that autonomy. Therefore, a modern state and human rights are mutually conditioned. Today in practically all societies, modern states have emerged with similar attributes—police, army, secret service, bureaucracy, etc. For the purposes of our research, it does not matter whether they

[13] "Most non-Western cultural and political traditions, like the pre-modern West, lacked not only the practice of human rights but also the very concept." J. Donnelly, *Universal Human Rights in Theory and Practice* (Ithaca: Cornell University Press, 1989), 50.

[14] Ibid., 70.

have imported these attributes from Western societies or have developed them on their own. What matters is whether, having introduced institutions that have the tendency, in the absence of proper guarantees in the form of democracy and human rights, not only to suppress individual freedoms but also to subordinate the whole society to the state apparatus, leaders of these states are free to cast democracy and human rights aside. Communitarian defenses of traditional practices usually cannot be extended to modern nation states and contemporary nationalist regimes,[15] and "constant references to communal society can be, and are, used to mask systematic violations of human rights in the interests of ruling elites."[16]

Fortunately, not all leaders of Asian or African countries are ignorant or hypocritical, and, what is especially important, Afro-Asian societies themselves are not so unreceptive to universal human rights as is asserted by some of their leaders. The fact that it is not so much the cultural phenomena or differences between societies, but rather the specific political interests of some of their ruling circles that form the basis for denying human rights in many countries was confirmed in the Bangkok Declaration on Human Rights adopted by 110 non-governmental organizations (NGOs) of Asia and the Pacific region on 27 March 1993.[17] The declaration stressed that "cultural practices which derogate from universally accepted human rights, including women's rights, must not be tolerated."[18] It is noteworthy that this is not the voice of Western NGOs. It is also significant that this document was adopted only a few days before the regional conference of official representatives of countries of Asia and the Pacific region, meeting in the same city, emphasized cultural relativism in its approach to human rights.

The fact that there are no inherently Western human rights standards can also be shown by tracing the roots of human rights, or rather their

[15] J. Donnelly, "Cultural Relativism and Universal Human Rights," *Human Rights Quarterly* 6 (1984), 411.

[16] Rhoda Howard, "Evaluating Human Rights in Africa: Some Problems of Implicit Comparisons," *Human Rights Quarterly* 6 (1984), 175.

[17] *Report of the Regional Meeting for Asia of the World Conference on Human Rights,* UN doc. A/CONF. 157/ASRM/8-A/CONF. 157/PC/59 (27 March 1993) (hereafter Bangkok NGO Declaration).

[18] Ibid., 1.

absence, in different religions, because religion is an important part of practically any culture. One should not be surprised by the findings of Adamantia Pollis, that in Orthodox theology "woman is considered morally inferior" or that the "inexorable conclusion . . . is that individual human rights cannot be derived from Orthodox theology."[19] What may be surprising is the underlying idea that human rights can derive to any degree from religion.

Though international human rights standards protect the freedom of religion and different religions or individual clergymen have often contributed to the protection of human rights, no religion in its fundamentalist form (which in terms of fundamentalists means, of course, the only true and genuine religion) is conducive to human rights. Even in a liberal institution such as the Church of England, the decision to allow the ordination of women, which from the human rights point of view is quite natural, was adopted far from unanimously in 1993 and has alienated many followers of the Church. Arthur Schlesinger, Jr., quite rightly observes:

> As an historian, I confess to a certain amusement when I hear the Judeo-Christian tradition praised as the source of our concern for human rights. In fact, the great religious ages were notable for their indifference to human rights in the contemporary sense. They were notorious not only for acquiescence in poverty, inequality, exploitation and oppression but for enthusiastic justifications of slavery, persecution, abandonment of small children, torture, genocide. Religion enshrined and vindicated hierarchy, authority and inequality.[20]

Cultural traditions of many societies contain elements that do not facilitate the implementation of human rights norms and some that are even conducive to the violation of rights. Rhoda Howard argues that "like the cultural underpinnings of most other societies, the cultural underpinnings of Western society do not all favour human rights."[21] Obviously, the Western philosophical and cultural traditions of social justice include not only

[19] Adamantia Pollis, "Eastern Orthodoxy and Human Rights," *Human Rights Quarterly* 15 (1993), 344, 353.

[20] Arthur Schlesinger Jr., "The Opening of the American Mind," *New York Times Book Review,* 23 July 1989, 26.

[21] Rhoda Howard, "Cultural Absolutism and the Nostalgia for Community," *Human Rights Quarterly* 15 (1993), 335.

liberalism but also communism, corporatism, racism, and fascism. This means that it is not culture as such, but rather certain cultural elements—which can be overcome without undermining the culture itself—that are contrary to human rights. Cultures are not immutable and become more civilized as they develop; the human rights component has an important role to play in this process.

Were it the people themselves of particular countries, rather than their leaders, who claim that universal human rights do not correspond to their traditional values, I would not insist on the universality of human rights. It would be an extreme folly to try to bring happiness, as understood by me or by those who think like me, to those who are already happy in their own way. But information coming from many Third World countries and reaching UN bodies such as the Human Rights Committee or the Commission on Human Rights, shows that these societies are not so unreceptive to universal human rights as their leaders or ideologues like to claim.

The Bangkok NGO Declaration indicates that Asian and Pacific societies, contrary to what some of their leaders say, do not think that human rights are imposed on them by Western societies. The declaration asserts, *inter alia,* that "violations of civil, political and economic rights frequently result from the emphasis on economic development at the expense of human rights"[22] and that "in many countries, suspects are tortured by law enforcement personnel [to extract] 'confessions.' This inhuman practice is officially encouraged by some authorities as a cheap and convenient method of crime control."[23] Therefore, the declaration calls on Asian-Pacific governments "to promote and protect the universality and indivisibility of human rights"[24] to "accede to and effectively implement international human rights instruments," and "to guarantee the totality of human rights."[25]

It is difficult to see any universal human rights norms that would be culturally unacceptable in some part of the world. Difficulties rooted in cultural or religious traditions may inhibit their full implementation in some societies, and it may be that a significant period of time will be needed to attain full compliance with these standards. Sometimes quite deeply

[22] Bangkok NGO Declaration, 1.

[23] Ibid., 4.

[24] Ibid., 9.

[25] Ibid., 11.

rooted traditions, which are inexcusable under universal human rights standards, cannot be eradicated immediately. India, for example, has not yet succeeded in completely eliminating such vestiges of the past as the "dowry death" (where a wife is killed because of the insufficiency of her dowry) or *sati* (where a widow is encouraged or forced to commit suicide after the death of her husband), but the government is undertaking legislative and administrative measures aimed at ending these crimes.[26] What is important is not the immediate planting of the whole range of human rights into an unprepared soil, which sometimes may lead to social unrest, but gradual and sincere efforts by governments to cultivate universal human rights standards. The UN Human Rights Committee, supervising the implementation of the International Covenant on Civil and Political Rights, always commends governments for progress made in implementing these rights, even if the situation in the country is still far from perfect (there is no paradise for human rights anywhere).

Moreover, universal human rights standards are not rigid rules in the sense that their interpretation and application cannot be adapted to different cultural traditions, even if some traditions at first glance seem to contradict these standards. For example, Article 23(3) of the International Covenant on Civil and Political Rights requires that "no marriage shall be entered into without the free and full consent of the intending spouses." Does this mean that a country in which marriages are arranged necessarily violates the covenant? I do not think so; if spouses themselves do not object to such marriages because of their society's age-old traditions, then this practice in itself does not contradict the covenant. The case would be quite different, of course, where young girls or boys are forced against their will to enter into marriage.

I think that it is possible in such cases to accept a compromise approach proposed by Rhoda Howard. She argues that instead of an outright ban of some of these practices (e.g., child betrothal, disinheritance of widows), it should be possible to "opt out" of such traditional practices in favor

[26] The new offence of "dowry death" was included in the Indian Penal Code; see also the Commission of Sati [Prevention] Act of 1987 (*Second Periodic Report of India to the UN Human Rights Committee,* UN doc. CCPR/C/137/Add. 13 [12 July 1989], paras. 117, 119).

of universal human rights.[27] Such an approach would encourage a gradual change of traditional practices in the light of universal human rights norms.

Certain deplorable practices can be eradicated only gradually, through purposeful, in particular, educational, measures. However, there are some practices that can never be reconciled with universal human rights norms, such as death for apostasy in some fundamentalist Islamic countries or the caste system and *sati* in India. Even today these practices are not only condemned by other value systems and universal human rights standards, but also find no unanimous support in their own cultural systems. Moreover, universal human rights norms, which help eradicate some cruel forms of punishment or treatment, do not undermine or impoverish the cultural foundations of societies in which such practices still occur. On the contrary, human rights norms can make these societies more humane. Human rights (or in some cases their violation) are in any case only one, albeit very important, part of culture.

All this seems to indicate that in cases of discrepancies between universal human rights standards, on the one hand, and practices that are rationalized by a specific cultural or religious tradition, on the other, the universal norm should prevail. This holds true even if leaders of some countries have signed universal human rights instruments or participated in human rights decisionmaking (possibly out of hypocrisy or ignorance).

The legal reasoning for such a conclusion is that fundamental human rights have become norms of international law, binding even for states that do not adhere to universal human rights instruments.[28] This conclusion is corroborated by the work of the UN Commission on Human Rights, which has often considered human rights situations countries that are not signatories to specific treaties (e.g., El Salvador, Cuba, Albania). The social and moral argument, which undoubtedly has legal significance, is that fundamental human rights and freedoms are claimed not solely by individuals from Western countries: Individuals and NGOs all over the world refer to universal human rights standards in support of their claims. The World

[27] Rhoda Howard, "Women's Rights in English-Speaking Sub-Saharan Africa," in C. Welch and R. Meltzer, eds., *Human Rights and Development in Africa* (Albany: State University of New York Press, 1984), 66–68.

[28] For example, A. D'Amato, *International Law: Process and Prospect* (New York: Transnational Publishers, 1987), 145.

Conference on Human Rights in June 1993 had good reason to emphasize that "all human rights are universal,[29] indivisible and interdependent and interrelated. The international community must treat human rights globally in a fair and equal manner, on the same footing, and with the same emphasis."[30]

The world community should monitor the human rights situation in all countries in light of international standards of human rights, taking into account underlying historical, social, economic, cultural, and religious factors. What is important is constant progress, not rapid, unprepared reforms that do not take these underlying realities into consideration.

Such an approach to human rights does not mean, however, that Musa bin Hitam, a leader of the Malaysian delegation to the 1993 Vienna World Conference on Human Rights is justified in saying that "each country is entitled to its own perception of human rights and forcing developing countries to follow the western perception is unfair and unjust."[31] Such an approach is an abuse of the problems and difficulties that stem from historical traditions and economic underdevelopment. My call for consideration of the social environment is directed to the international community of states and special monitoring bodies; I am not preparing excuses for governments of those states that hide behind difficulties, often created by themselves, to excuse their poor human rights records.

The UN Human Rights Committee, for example, always appreciates the genuine efforts of all states, and especially of Third World countries, which often face real difficulties in implementing the International Covenant on Civil and Political Rights. It knows which states have not yet achieved full implementation of the covenant despite real efforts. Governments that hide behind the outdated non-interference concept and try to explain away their problems by invoking historical, cultural, or religious

[29] Not all human rights are, in my view, universal; there are certainly rights which are national or regional. Fundamental or basic human rights, however, are universal, or, though it may sound tautological, we may say that all universal human rights are universal.

[30] *Declaration and Programme of Action,* UN doc. A/CONF. 157/23 (12 July 1993), Section I, para. 5.

[31] K. Cooke, "Asians Challenge West on Human Rights," *Financial Times,* 11 June 1993.

traditions and economic underdevelopment often simply have not undertaken even gradual efforts to implement international human rights standards. Rhoda Howard argues that "many human rights-abusive practices that do exist are not intrinsic to the culture; rather they are consequences of economic and political interest."[32] Often governments deny human beings under their jurisdiction universal human rights, not for the sake of the well-being of the population but in order to stay in power.

Human rights are conditioned by three factors: anthropological, societal, and international. These factors, or at least the latter two, are not immutable in time and space. While societal factors—those that pertain to the characteristics of a given society, including its culture—have exercised the strongest influence on the content of the rights and freedoms of members of the society, international factors, though of more recent origin, are growing in their influence. Some rights, like the right to life, the right to freedom from torture, and the right to establish a family, are anthropological, though like all rights, they can exist only in society; Robinson Crusoe had no rights or obligations before the appearance of Friday.

The growing interdependence of the world as a whole and the penetrability of most societies mean that international factors, through purposeful efforts as well as through simple osmosis, are influencing human rights concepts and practices. Fundamental human rights and freedoms are inalienable not because they are inviolable or because they are universally observed; were this so, there would be no need for human rights. They are inalienable because mankind at this stage of its development has recognized them as inalienable and has confirmed this, *inter alia,* by giving them the status of rights and freedoms of all human beings under international law. This, however, does not and should not lead to a global cultural uniformity.

It may be true that for some countries certain rights may seem more important than others. Musa bin Hitam has said that "Malaysia views development as very basic to human rights" and that "civil and political rights should come almost automatically after development has been achieved."[33] Nonetheless, even if some countries, such as Malaysia, view development

[32] R. Howard, "Cultural Absolutism and Nostalgia for Community," *Human Rights Quarterly* 15 (1993), 337.

[33] Cooke, "Asians Challenge West."

as a basic human right, this does not mean that if development is guaranteed civil and political rights will automatically follow or that limitations on civil and political rights are necessary to secure development.

When the Soviet Union's human rights record was criticized it was not because that nation put social and economic rights first and considered them more important than civil and political rights. The socialist concept of human rights, as something different from and even "higher" than the so-called Western concept, was used to conceal real human rights abuses in the Soviet Union and other so-called socialist states. These regimes treated human rights not as a practical problem but as an ideological one. The lack of civil and political rights was one of the reasons for the stagnation of the Soviet Union's economy and consequently for the poor state of social and economic rights. This means that—at least at a certain level of development—progress can be achieved not at the expense of civil and political rights but only through their full observance.

The recent history of some rapidly developing countries—the "small tigers" of east Asia and Chile under Pinochet—demonstrates that democracy is not a *conditio sine qua non* for economic growth. Frances Stewart even argues that "a more liberal political system may be incapable of producing and sustaining the reorientation in the economy necessary for these types of successes."[34]

At the same time, while democracy is not always a precondition for rapid economic growth, most dictatorships do not prosper economically. It is unlikely that limitations on democracy and human rights in South Korea, Malaysia, and Singapore, or massive repressions in Chile under Pinochet contributed in any way to the economic growth of these countries. Moreover, a strong executive power is not by any means tantamount to a repressive regime. Jack Donnelly argues that "a blanket trade-off of civil and political rights, whatever its economic effects, unjustifiably ignores the manifest diversity of these rights. For example, torture, disappearances, and arbitrary executions can almost always be eliminated with no cost to development."[35] He is right to point out that the extensive use of particularly brutal forms of torture during Park Chung Hee's last years in South Korea

[34] F. Stewart, *Basic Needs in Developing Countries* (Baltimore: Johns Hopkins University Press, 1985), 212.

[35] Donnelly, *Universal Human Rights in Theory and Practice,* 201–2.

had nothing to do with development; if anything, repression in the late 1970s hindered development.[36] The "necessity" of "developmental repression" lies largely in the realm of politics, not economics.[37] The tendency toward political liberalization in South Korea in the 1990s has been dictated, *inter alia,* by economic considerations. The *Economist* notes that "as Asian countries move towards rich-world income levels, their appetite for multi-party politics seems to grow."[38] One may nonetheless agree with the former prime minister of Singapore, Lee Kuan Yu, that it is much easier for a nation in that part of the world to enrich itself economically than to reach a stage where its society is ready for full democracy.[39]

On the other hand, the experience of Mobutu Sese Seko, Idi Amin, Jean-Bedel Bokassa, and a host of other dictators shows convincingly how a strong government may become not a remedy but a disaster, both for a country's human rights record and for its economy. Gross human rights violations by authorities in countries such as Sri Lanka, India, and Peru play into the hands of terrorist organizations, helping them to recruit new members. Therefore, I agree with Robert Bartley when he writes that "the dominant flow of historical forces in the 21st century could well be this: economic development leads to demands for democracy and individual (or family) autonomy; instant worldwide communications reduce the power of oppressive governments; the spread of democratic states diminishes the potential for conflict."[40]

Moreover, economic growth and social stability are not the only things that matter. "While development facilitates the enjoyment of all human rights, the lack of development may not be invoked to justify the abridgment of internationally recognised human rights."[41] In our world it has become impossible to remain indulgent of dictators, even if their countries prosper economically. The end of the Cold War has made it even more

[36] Ibid., 189.

[37] Ibid., 188.

[38] *Economist,* 30 October 1993, Asia Survey, 23.

[39] Ibid.

[40] R. L. Bartley, "The Case for Optimism: The West Should Believe in Itself," *Foreign Affairs* 72 (1993), 17.

[41] UN doc. A/CONF. 157/23, Section I, para. 5.

difficult to close one's eyes to gross violations of human rights and to retain normal diplomatic and trade relations with regimes that do not guarantee basic human rights.

At the same time, the lack of social and economic rights, which in essence is tantamount to gross social inequality and injustice, is one of the main causes of violations of civil and political rights in many countries. Civil-political and socio-economic rights are not only in themselves equally important categories of human rights; the denial of these rights is a serious cause of social unrest, which, in turn, is met with repression by many governments. Zehra Arat argues convincingly that "the decline of democracy and the transition to authoritarian rule in developing countries are attributable to politics that create an imbalance between the two groups of human rights, civil and political rights and socioeconomic rights, by ignoring the latter group. The increasing gap between the two groups of rights . . . causes frustration and social unrest, which in turn is suppressed by coercive politics."[42]

Social unrest, often leading to political repression, may not only be caused by ineffective and corrupt economic management. Even rapid economic development, if the latter is accompanied by gross social inequalities and neglect of social and economic rights, may lead to a political crisis. The revolutions in Mexico, Cuba, and Nicaragua took place following a period of economic growth, not stagnation, but that economic growth was very uneven.[43] The revolt of the southern Mexican state of Chiapas should be a warning not only to the Mexican government. Arat rightly observes that "stable democracy tends to reflect higher levels of socioeconomic equality. The neglect of social and economic rights puts pressure on the system and eventually leads the civil and political rights that are the ingredients of a viable democracy to draw a declining curve."[44]

The relationship between economic development and democracy is complicated and non-linear. It may be that in certain societies at certain periods of their socioeconomic or political development, "enlightened au-

[42] Z. F. Arat, *Democracy and Human Rights in Developing Countries* (London: Lynne Rienner Publishers, 1991), 9.

[43] Ibid., 81.

[44] Ibid., 56.

thoritarian" regimes guarantee higher rates of economic growth. Even in such cases, however, gross and systematic human rights violations (e.g., torture, disappearances, arbitrary arrests) have nothing to do with the speed of development. On the other hand, neglect of social and economic rights, which in itself may constitute the gross and systematic violation of human rights, is one of the causes of the eventual suppression of civil and political rights in many developing countries.

One of the threats not only to human rights in some societies but to the international system as a whole comes from Islamic fundamentalism.[45] Paul Kennedy argues that "far from preparing for the twenty-first century, much of the Arab and Muslim world appears to have difficulty in coming to terms with the nineteenth century, with its composite legacy of secularisation, democracy, laissez-faire economics, transnational industrial and commercial linkages, social change, and intellectual questioning. If one needed an example of the importance of cultural attitudes in explaining a society's response to change, contemporary Islam provides it."[46] Frances Fukuyama points out that "part of the current, fundamentalist revival is the strength of the perceived threat from liberal, Western values to traditional Islamic societies."[47] If this is so, then the spread of liberal democracies should in the foreseeable future further consolidate Islamic fundamentalism.

Terrorism and gross human rights violations are almost inevitable concomitants of any religious or ideological fundamentalism, especially when it becomes clear that the fundamentalism is leading to a dead end. There-

[45] Hindu fundamentalism, though confined essentially to one country, may be as damaging as Islamic fundamentalism. It seems astonishing at the end of the twentieth century, to read words like those uttered by Sardar Angre, an adviser to one of the founders of the extreme right wing pro-Hindu Bharatiya Janata Party (BJP), Rajmata Vijayaraje Scindia: "The Muslims must be made to understand that they must be proud of Hindustan. . . . If the Muslims followed the Hindu ideology there would be no more trouble. . . . They should accept our common culture and unite with us in the name of god." *Sunday Times Magazine* (London), 9 May 1993, 51. This is an exact recipe for an inter-religious conflict and, consequently, for gross human rights violations.

[46] Paul Kennedy, *Preparing for the Twenty-First Century* (London: HarperCollins, 1993), 208.

[47] F. Fukuyama, *The End of History and the Last Man* (London: Hamish Hamilton, 1992), 46.

fore, Islamic fundamentalism will remain a serious threat to regional and even world stability, and it undermines the very essence of human rights in those Muslim societies where fundamentalists are in power or influence social and political life in the country.

I will not enter into detailed comparisons of *Shari'a* with universal human rights standards. It is well treated in works written by Muslim authors who are familiar with the problem from the inside.[48] Nonetheless, periodic reports concerning Sudan and Iran[49] by the UN Human Rights Committee have revealed serious inconsistencies between Islamic law and practice and the International Covenant on Civil and Political Rights. These inconsistencies have occurred in three basic areas: equality between men and women, freedom of conscience and religion, and prohibition of cruel treatment or punishment. The report on human rights in Iran of Reynaldo Galindo Pohl, Special Representative of the Commission on Human Rights, referred in particular to the high number of executions, cases of torture and cruel, inhuman or degrading treatment or punishment, and discriminatory treatment of certain groups of citizens—notably the Baha'is—on the basis of their religious beliefs.[50] The situation in these crucial areas inevitably leads to the violation of other rights, such as freedom of association or the right to life. Abdullahi Ahmed An-Na'im argues that "by granting women and non-Muslims a lower status and sanctioning discriminatory treatment against them, Shari'a denies women and non-Muslims the same degree of honour and human dignity it guarantees to Muslim men."[51] Cruel forms of punishment provided for in some countries under *Shari'a,* as well as treatment of apostasy as a crime, are other practices that are manifestly contrary to universal human rights norms.

Certainly, it is not realistic to hope to eradicate such deplorable practices overnight. On the other hand, though these practices are rooted in religion and custom, they are no longer unreservedly accepted by all Muslims. In the Bangkok Declaration, 110 non-governmental organizations from Asia and the Pacific region, where many countries are Muslim, call on

48 See, for example, An-Na'im, *Human Rights.*

49 See, for example, UN doc. CCPR/C/SR.1253 (30 July 1993).

50 UN doc. E/CN.4/1993/41 (28 January 1993).

51 A. A. An-Na'im, *Toward an Islamic Reformation: Civil Liberties, Human Rights, and International Law* (Syracuse, N.Y.: Syracuse University Press, 1990), 163.

all governments of the region to ratify basic UN human rights documents, in particular the Convention on the Elimination of All Forms of Discrimination Against Women (CEDAW), and to withdraw reservations, particularly those applying to CEDAW and the Convention on the Rights of Children. The Bangkok Declaration also calls for the abolishment of the death penalty.[52] Are not such views from those countries where specific violations of human rights take place the strongest indicators that the world community cannot accept cultural and religious peculiarities as an excuse for these practices? During the consideration of the Iranian report in the UN Human Rights Committee, the Iranian representative claimed, *inter alia,* that women themselves wished to wear traditional clothing, including the veil. Members of the committee rightly questioned this assertion: "that desire must be very moderate in the extreme if authorities needed to resort to death sentences and raids by militia in order to secure women's compliance with that requirement."[53] The committee also emphasized that "women who did not wish to change [their dress or lifestyle] should not be forced to do so, but it was quite wrong to threaten and penalize those women who were desirous of change."[54]

As I have stated above, any religious fundamentalism leads to a dead end. An-Na'im argues that "toleration of unorthodoxy and dissent is vital for the spiritual and intellectual benefit of Islam itself."[55] He continues: "It is my conviction as a Muslim that the public law of Shari'a does not represent the law of Islam which contemporary Muslims are supposed to implement in fulfilment of their religious obligation. I also strongly believe that the application of the public law of Shari'a today will be counterproductive and detrimental to Muslims and to Islam itself."[56] Unfortunately, in some Muslim countries, the government's struggle against fundamentalists is often conducted in violation of human rights. The Algerian authorities at the beginning of 1992 used undemocratic means to prevent forces that they considered hostile to democracy from taking advantage of democratic

[52] Bangkok NGO Declaration, 10–11.

[53] UN doc. CCPR/C/SR.1253, 7.

[54] Ibid., 10.

[55] An-Na'im, *Islamic Reformation,* 184.

[56] Ibid., 187.

procedures.[57] As a result of these measures, some 3,000 people have been killed in violence, and more than 360 militants have been sentenced to death.[58] These measures, in turn, have led to the slaughter by Muslim fundamentalists of foreigners in Algeria. Governmental repression has further radicalized fundamentalists who "make it plain that the FIS [Islamic Salvation Front] no longer speaks on their behalf"[59]; terrorists threaten to kill anyone who negotiates with the government.[60] This experience, as well as that in other Muslim countries, shows that the use of repression is not the way to deal with religious fundamentalism; it may lead to a new cycle of violence that inevitably undermines basic human rights in the society as a whole. Here, the experience in Jordan, where King Hussein sought to bring Islamic parties into the political system, has been much more successful.[61] Fundamentalists have much stronger positions in countries where governments are ineffective and corrupt. If not religious fundamentalism itself, then at least its rise in many countries is a counterreaction not only to Western influence but to domestic corruption and repression as well.

[57] See, for example, the consideration of the Algerian initial report in the UN Human Rights Committee. UN doc. A/47/40 (9 October 1992), 69–77.

[58] *Economist,* 27 November 1993, 74.

[59] *Economist,* 18 December 1993, 56.

[60] *Economist,* 18 December 1993, 56.

[61] *Times* (London), 17 December 1993, 21.

Notes on the Contributors

Lori Fisler Damrosch, a professor of law at Columbia University, is a lawyer and legal scholar with teaching experience in such areas as public international law, the Constitution and US foreign affairs, international institutions, enforcing international law, law and foreign intelligence, East-West trade, and transnational litigation. She has held positions with the Office of the Legal Adviser in the US Department of State and also in private practice. Professor Damrosch has been published extensively, including, as editor, *Enforcing Restraint: Collective Intervention in Internal Conflicts* (New York, 1993).

Mahbub ul Haq is president of the Human Development Centre in Pakistan. Until recently, he served as special adviser to the administrator of the United Nations Development Programme (UNDP) and chief architect of the UNDP's annual *Human Development Report*. Founder of the Third World Forum in 1973, Dr. Haq was chairman of the North-South Roundtable (1979–1984) and an adviser to the Brandt Commission (1980–1982). Dr. Haq was also governor of the International Monetary Fund (1985) and the World Bank (1988). Prior to that, he was chief economist of the Pakistan Planning Commission (1957–1970) and director of the World Bank's Policy Planning Department (1970–1982). From 1982 to 1988, he was planning and finance minister in Pakistan's federal cabinet. His major publications include *Strategy of Economic Planning* (Karachi, 1966), *The Poverty Curtain* (New York, 1976), *Sustainable Development: From Concept to Action* (New York, 1992), and, as co-editor, *Reflections on Human Development* (New York, 1995).

Louis Henkin is University Professor Emeritus at the Columbia University School of Law. Before his appointment, he held chairs in constitutional law and, earlier, in international law and diplomacy. Educated at Yeshiva College and Harvard Law School, Professor Henkin served as law clerk to Judge Learned Hand and Justice Felix Frankfurter and was an officer of the US Department of State before turning to academic life. He served as the chief reporter of the *Restatement of Foreign Relations Law of the United States* (1979–1987) and as co-editor-in-chief of the *American Journal of International Law* (1978–1984). From 1992 to 1994, he was president of the American Society of International Law. He is the author of numerous books and articles, including *Foreign Affairs and the U.S. Constitution* (Oxford-New York, 1990; 2d ed., 1996), *The Age of Rights* (New York, 1990; rev. ed., 1996), and *Constitutionalism, Democracy, and Foreign Affairs* (New York, 1990).

Michael Howard is Professor Emeritus of Oxford University, where he held the Regius Chair of Modern History from 1980 to 1989, and of Yale University, where he was Robert A. Lovett Professor of Military and Naval History from 1989 to 1993. He is a Fellow of the British Academy and a Foreign Corresponding Member of the American Academy of Arts and Sciences. He was responsible for the foundation both of the Department of War Studies at King's College, London, where he held the chair of war studies from 1963 to 1968, and the International Institute for Strategic Studies, of which he is honorary life president. His publications include *The Franco-Prussian War* (London-New York, 1961), *War in European History* (London-New York, 1976), and *War and the Liberal Conscience* (New Brunswick, N.J., 1978). With Peter Paret he translated Carl von Clausewitz's *On War* (Princeton, 1976; rev. ed., 1984).

Dorothy V. Jones is a scholar-in-residence at the Newberry Library, Chicago, and a history department associate at Northwestern University. An independent scholar, she is a member of the Board of Trustees of the Carnegie Council on Ethics and International Affairs and serves on the editorial advisory board of the council's journal. A contributor to several recent volumes on international affairs, she is also the author of *Code of Peace* (Chicago), which won the 1991 Lionel Gelber prize for the best book on international relations published that year. She holds a Ph.D. in US diplomatic history from the University of Chicago.

Karl Kaiser is the director of the Research Institute of the German Society for Foreign Affairs and professor of political science at the University of Bonn. Professor Kaiser served previously as research associate and lecturer at Harvard University, where he has returned several times as a visiting professor. In 1993, he received an honorary doctorate from the Russian Academy of Sciences. He was a member of the Council of Environmental Advisers of the Federal Republic of Germany and of the Government Commission for the Reform of the Armed Services. He is the recipient of the Prix Adolphe Bentinck and the Atlantic Award. His many books include *German Foreign Policy in Transition* (London, 1968), *Europe and the United States* (Washington, D.C., 1973), and *Die neue Weltpolitik* (Bonn, 1995).

Walid Khalidi has been a senior research associate at the Center for Middle East Studies at Harvard University since 1982. His appointments prior to this include the positions of visiting professor of government at Harvard University, professor of political studies at the American University of Beirut, and university lecturer at Oxford University. Dr. Khalidi is vice-chairman of the Academic Advisory Board at the Center for Muslim-Christian Understanding at Georgetown University and is a Fellow of the American Academy of Arts and Sciences. He has lectured extensively on topics ranging from Middle East politics to nuclear proliferation, conflict resolution, and intercultural attitudes. Dr. Khalidi has published many articles in leading Arabic dailies and periodicals, as well as in other international newspapers and foreign affairs journals. He is the author of several books, including *Conflict and Violence in Lebanon* (Cambridge, Mass., 1979), *All That Remains* (Washington, D.C., 1992), and *Palestine Reborn* (London-New York, 1992).

Angeliki E. Laiou is director of Dumbarton Oaks in Washington, D.C. Since 1981, she has held the position of Dumbarton Oaks Professor of Byzantine History at Harvard University. Previously she had been on the faculty of Rutgers University as a Distinguished Professor. Professor Laiou has been the recipient of grants and fellowships from Harvard University, the American Council of Learned Societies, and the Guggenheim Foundation, and has been elected Fellow of the Medieval Academy of America and Fellow of the American Academy of Arts and Sciences. Her research has concentrated on diplomatic, social, and economic history. Her recent publications include *Marriage, amour et parenté à Byzance, XI–XIIIème* *siècles* (Paris, 1992) and, as co-editor, *Law and Society in Byzantium, Ninth-Twelfth Centuries* (Washington, D.C., 1994).

Ernest Richard May teaches in the Department of History and at the John F. Kennedy School of Government at Harvard University. He has been a professor of history since 1963 and the Charles Warren Professor of History since 1981. From 1969 to 1972, he was dean of Harvard College and associate dean of the Faculty of Arts and Sciences. He was director of the Institute of Politics from 1971 to 1974 and chairman of the Department of History from 1976 to 1979. Professor May has been a consultant at various times to the Office of the Secretary of Defense, the National Security Council, the Lawrence Livermore National Laboratory, the National Endowment for the Humanities, the Smithsonian Institution, and committees of the US Congress. Widely published, his most recent publication is *American Cold War Strategy: Interpreting NSC 68* (Boston, 1993).

Rein Müllerson is professor of international law at King's College, London. Prior to this position, he was Centennial Professor of International Law at the London School of Economics and Political Science. He has also served as deputy foreign minister of the Republic of Estonia and head of the Estonian delegation to the human dimension conferences in Geneva and Moscow of the Conference on Security and Co-operation in Europe. He has lectured on sources of international law at the Institute of International Law and International Relations in Saloniki, Greece, and taught courses on international law at Moscow State University. Professor Müllerson has published more than one hundred articles on international law and politics and is the author of *International Law, Rights and Politics* (London-New York, 1994), *Beyond Confrontation: International Law for the Post-Cold War Era* (Boulder, Colo., 1995), and *Human Rights Diplomacy* (London-New York, 1997).

Alain Pellet is professor of public international law at the University of Paris X—Nanterre and at the Institute for Political Science in Paris. Since 1990, he has been a member of the International Law Commission of the United Nations. Mr. Pellet has also been counsel for various states before the International Court of Justice. Widely published, he is the editor of an article-by-article commentary on the UN Charter, soon to be published in English.

Vladimir Petrovsky, currently the director-general of the United Nations Office in Geneva, began his foreign service career in 1957 as a staff member of the Permanent Mission of the Soviet Union to the United Nations. During his career, he has held such positions as deputy foreign minister and first deputy foreign minister of the Soviet Union and under-secretary-general for political affairs at the United Nations. Mr. Petrovsky has published many articles and books, including *Vneshniaia politika SShA: Teoreticheskii arsenal* (US foreign policy: Theoretical arsenal) (Moscow, 1973), *Doktrina "natsional'noi bezopasnosti" v global'noi strategii SShA* (The doctrine of national security in the US global strategy) (Moscow, 1980), and *The Soviet Concept of Disarmament* (Moscow, 1984).

Indar Jit Rikhye is senior research associate in the Program on Peace-keeping Policy at George Mason University's Institute on Public Policy. Previously, he was a senior adviser for United Nations Affairs at the United States Institute of Peace, where he conducted several projects on ways to strengthen UN peacekeeping. A retired major-general in the Indian army, Mr. Rikhye has spent the past thirty-five years working in the area of multilateral peacekeeping as a diplomat, soldier, and educator. Following the 1956 Suez War, he served in Gaza as a unit commander and later as chief of staff for the first UN peacekeeping mission. As military adviser to Secretaries-General Dag Hammarskjöld and U Thant, he led peacekeeping operations in the Congo, West Irian, the Dominican Republic, Yemen, and Gaza. In 1969, he founded the International Peace Academy. Mr. Rikhye is the author or co-author of many articles and several books, including *Military Adviser to the Secretary-General: U.N. Peacekeeping and the Congo Crisis* (London-New York, 1993). In 1985, UNESCO awarded him its Prize for Peace Education.

Neil L. Rudenstine is president of Harvard University. Before assuming this position in 1991, he served for three years as executive vice president of the Andrew W. Mellon Foundation. During the two preceding decades, Mr. Rudenstine was a faculty member and senior administrator at Princeton University, where he served as a professor of English and as dean of students (1968–1972), dean of the college (1972–1977), and provost (1977–1988). A scholar of Renaissance literature, Mr. Rudenstine is an honorary Fellow of New College, Oxford, and a Fellow of the American

Academy of Arts and Sciences. He is also a member of the Council on Foreign Relations, the American Philosophical Society, and the Committee for Economic Development.

Henry Trofimenko is currently chief analyst with the United States and Canada Institute of the Russian Academy of Sciences. From 1974 to 1991 he headed the institute's department for the study of US foreign policy. In 1989 he was awarded the title of Honorary Scholar of the Russian Federation by the Presidium of the Supreme Soviet of Russia. Mr. Trofimenko has served as a visiting professor at such schools as Barnard College, Elon College, the School of International Service at American University, and at the Center for International Security Studies at the University of Maryland. In 1994 he was a senior research associate at the International Security Council in Washington, D.C. He has been a regular participant in seminars on the problems of change in the former Soviet Union at Columbia University, the Brookings Institution, the Institute for Policy Studies, and the RAND Corporation. He also is the author and contributor to more than thirty books on international relations, Soviet and US foreign policy, and arms control.

Brian Urquhart was scholar-in-residence for the International Affairs Program of the Ford Foundation from 1986 to 1996, following his retirement from the UN Secretariat. As under-secretary-general for Special Political Affairs, his main functions were the direction of peacekeeping forces and conflict control negotiations. Mr. Urquhart has written a number of books on international affairs, including biographies of Dag Hammarskjöld (New York, 1972) and Ralph Bunche (New York, 1993).

Zi Zhongyun is senior fellow and former director of the Institute of American Studies at the Chinese Academy of Social Sciences and editor-in-chief of *Meiguo Yanjiu (Journal of American Studies in China).* She is also the president of the Society for Chinese Scholars of Sino-US Relations, a member of the Executive Committee of the Chinese Association of American Studies, and a member of the Standing Committee of the Society for Pacific Affairs. Professor Zi has been published extensively and is the author of several books and a series of articles about international relations, foreign policy, and East-West culture. She was a visiting professor at Beijing

University and Nanjing University–Johns Hopkins University Center for Chinese and American Studies. She has been awarded the title Scholar of Outstanding Contribution to the Nation.

Honorary Committee*

Dumbarton Oaks Conference, 1944–1994

Hélène Ahrweiler, President, Université de l'Europe
Anatolii F. Dobrynin, Counselor to the Foreign Ministry of the Russian Federation
James P. Grant, Executive Director, UNICEF; UN Under-Secretary-General
Mahbub ul Haq, Special Adviser to the United Nations Development Programme Administrator
Karl Kaiser, Director of the Research Institute of the German Society for Foreign Affairs; Professor of Political Science, University of Bonn
Nancy Landon Kassebaum, US Senator
Laurence Martin, Director, The Royal Institute of International Affairs
Nobuo Matsunaga, President and Director, The Japan Institute of International Affairs
Jagat Mehta, President, Seva Mandir; Professor, Lyndon B. Johnson School of Public Affairs, University of Texas at Austin
Dominique Moisi, Deputy Director, Institut Français des Relations Internationales
Daniel Patrick Moynihan, US Senator
Sadako Ogata, United Nations High Commissioner for Refugees
Mario Ojeda-Gómez, President, El Colegio de México
Olara Otunnu, President, International Peace Academy
James B. Reston[†], Author and Journalist, *The New York Times*
Neil L. Rudenstine, President, Harvard University
Paul Sarbanes, US Senator
George P. Shultz, Distinguished Fellow, Hoover Institution, Stanford University; US Secretary of State, 1982–1989
William Royall Tyler, Director, Dumbarton Oaks, 1969–1977
Cyrus Vance, Partner, Simpson, Thacher and Bartlett; US Secretary of State, 1977–1980
Zi Zhongyun, Senior Fellow, Institute of American Studies, Chinese Academy of Social Sciences

*Affiliations are at the time of the conference.

Program

Dumbarton Oaks Conference, 1944–1994

5–7 May 1994

Department of State, 5 May

Douglas J. Bennet, Assistant Secretary of State for International Organization Affairs
Keynote Address on the Fiftieth Anniversary of the Dumbarton Oaks Conversations

Dumbarton Oaks, 6 May

Opening Remarks

Neil L. Rudenstine, President, Harvard University
Angeliki E. Laiou, Director, Dumbarton Oaks

Session I: On the Expectations of 1944–1945

Moderator: Shirley Williams, Project Liberty, Kennedy School of Government, Harvard University

Michael Howard, Oxford and Yale Universities
The United Nations: From War Fighting to Peace Planning

Dorothy V. Jones, Newberry Library
Sober Expectations: The United Nations and a "Sensible Machinery" for Peace

Henry Trofimenko, International Security Council
Hope That Is Gradually Coming True

Zi Zhongyun, Institute of American Studies, Chinese Academy of Social Sciences
Big Power Assurance of Peace Versus the Principle of Equality among All Nations

Session II: On the Realities of the Postwar Climate

Moderator: Akira Iriye, Department of History, Harvard University

Karl Kaiser, Research Institute of the German Society for Foreign Affairs and the University of Bonn

Lessons of the Postwar Experience in Europe

Walid Khalidi, Center for Middle Eastern Studies, Harvard University

The Peacekeeping Role of the UN in the Cold War: A Middle Eastern and Third World Perspective

Nobuo Matsunaga, The Japan Institute of International Affairs

Fifty Years after the Dumbarton Oaks Expectations: A View from Asia

Luncheon Address, Dumbarton Oaks Gardens, North Vista

Brian Urquhart, International Affairs Program, The Ford Foundation

The Developing Role of the Secretary-General

Session III: International Institutions and International Security

Moderator: Bryan Hehir, Harvard Divinity School and the Harvard Center for International Affairs

Lori F. Damrosch, School of Law, Columbia University

Collective Economic Sanctions: Nonforcible Responses to Threats to Peace

Stanley Hoffmann, Center for European Studies, Harvard University

International Institutions and Intervention

Indar Jit Rikhye, United States Institute of Peace

Peacekeeping Operations

Session IV: Issues of Economic Development and the Environment
Moderator: Jessica T. Mathews, Council on Foreign Relations

Mahbub ul Haq, Special Adviser to the UN Development Programme Administrator
Humanizing Global Institutions

Michael B. McElroy, Department of Earth and Planetary Sciences, Harvard University
Scientific Perspectives on a Changing Environment

Jean Ripert, Adviser to the French Foreign Ministry on Sustainable Development
Changes in Approaches and Policies of Industrial Countries: More Urgent than Institutional Reform of the UN System

Dumbarton Oaks, 7 May
Session V: International Institutions, the Media, and the College Curriculum
Moderator and Speaker: Ernest May, Kennedy School of Government, Harvard University

Hélène Ahrweiler, Université de l'Europe
Universities and International Relations

Karen Breslau, *Newsweek*

Lisa Martin, Department of Government, Harvard University
International Institutions, the Media, and the College Curriculum: A Political Scientist's Perspective

Jagat Mehta, Seva Mandir
International Institutions, Media, and Communications

Commentators: Ralph Begleiter, CNN, and Richard Ullman, Woodrow Wilson School of Public and International Affairs, Princeton University

Session VI: Human Rights and Refugees
Moderator: Abram Chayes, Harvard Law School, Harvard University

Abdullahi An-Na'im, Human Rights Watch/Africa Watch
Beyond the Relativity/Universality Debate: Toward a Global Human Rights Culture

Louis Henkin, School of Law, Columbia University
Human Rights and State Sovereignty: A Half Century after Dumbarton Oaks

Rein Müllerson, London School of Economics and Political Science
Universal Human Rights in the Multicultural World

Alain Pellet, University of Paris X—Nanterre
Individual Rights, Minority Rights, and Group Rights

Session VII: The Future: Capabilities and Limitations of International Institutions and Organizations
Moderator: Joseph S. Nye, Jr., National Intelligence Council

Tom Farer, Washington College of Law and School of International Service, American University
Managing a Disorderly Global Society: What Role for the United Nations and Regional Organizations?

Nancy Landon Kassebaum, R–Kansas, US Senate

Peter Leuprecht, Council of Europe
The Future: Learning the Lessons of the Past: Reflections of a European

Mario Ojeda-Gómez, El Colegio de México
The Developing Countries and the New International Context

Vladimir Petrovsky, United Nations Office, Geneva*
Strategic Triad of the New Era

Paul Sarbanes, D–Maryland, US Senate

*Represented by Albrecht G. Muth, personal representative of Vladimir Petrovsky